THE
## COASTLINE
SERIES

# SOUTH CORNISH HARBOURS

## Liz Luck

### Illustrated by Rosemary Robertson

NAUTICAL

First published in Great Britain by
Nautical Books
an imprint of A & C Black (Publishers) Ltd
35 Bedford Row, London, WC1R 4JH

© Liz Luck 1988

ISBN 07136 5750 2

**British Library Cataloguing in Publication Data**
Luck, Liz
    South Cornish harbours.—(Coastline series)
    1. Cornwall. South Cornwall. Harbours
    I. Title    II. Series
387.1′094237

## ACKNOWLEDGEMENTS

Many thanks to the following people for giving me their help, advice and information:
Leslie Douch and Angela Broome of the Royal Institution of Cornwall; the staff of St.
Austell and Fowey libraries; the staff of the Harbour Office, Newlyn; Captain Wilson,
Fowey Harbourmaster; Mr. Rafferty, Mevagissey Harbourmaster; Oliver Padel; Jan
Channell; J. C. Trewin; Lamorna Kerr; Doreen Varcoe; Ross Carter; Martin Pumphrey;
David Carey; Mary Potter; Bud for showing me the brickworks; Rosemary for enduring
the cold and wet and still drawing so wonderfully; James Mildren for putting me up to it;
Janet Shearer for making me do it; Citroen for making my car; Mum for driving me
everywhere after it packed up.

Thanks also to the following for permission to reproduce passages from the publications
specified:
A. L. Rowse and Faber & Faber Ltd. (*Poems Chiefly Cornish* by A. L. Rowse); Faber &
Faber Ltd. (*Cornwall, A Shell Guide* by John Betjeman); Dyllansow Truran and Barbara
Fox (*Helford River* by C. C. Vyvyan); Peter Dalwood and Barbara Fox (*The Old Place* by
C. C. Vyvyan); The West Briton Newspaper Co. Ltd. (numerous extracts from *The West
Briton*); Royal Cornwall Polytechnic Society (Stanhope Forbes Address in 1900 Report);
Cambridge University Press (*From a Cornish Window* and *Memories and Opinions* by
Arthur Quiller Couch); Bossiney Books (essay by J. C. Trewin in *Both Sides of the Tamar*);
Jack Clemo and Methuen and Co. Ltd. (*The Echoing Tip* by Jack Clemo); Methuen and Co.
Ltd. (*Walking in Cornwall* by J. R. A. Hockin); Victor Gollancz and Lady Browning
(*Frenchman's Creek* and *Vanishing Cornwall* by Daphne du Maurier); Anthony Mott Ltd.
(*Twenty Years at St. Hilary* by Bernard Walke).

## Foreword

As you might expect in a near-island county where inland communications barely existed until the last century, Cornwall's eyes have long been turned upon the water. All Cornish life once revolved around it, unconsciously, naturally. Throughout history the main thoroughfares of everyday life here have been the coastal waters and the great navigable rivers of the south coast which burrow deep into remote rural Cornwall, bringing a seaweed smell to broadleaved woods in valleys far inland. A network of ancient paths and tracks links every old farm with its nearest tidal water, and a farm with direct river access and a quay of its own was always considered to be worth twice as much as a land-bound estate until road transport began to take the place of water.

The tumbled quay beside a long-silted creek, the grim and secretive fishing village crouched behind a stumpy wall, the deep-water estuarine port with an elegance of cranes and warehouses and great ships – these are all Cornish harbours. Some have a history of national importance – a great trading port of Medieval England, a major source of ships for the royal wars, a haven renowned throughout Europe for piracy and lawlessness – whilst others played out their role on a smaller stage, but no less significant were they to the slow shaping of Cornwall and the lives of Cornish people.

Things have changed dramatically in just the last fifty years or so. The central influence of the sea on ordinary life has retreated almost to the point of complete disappearance, perhaps for ever. Increasingly the rivers and coastal waters take on a peripheral role and are used for recreation only. But beneath the gloss of leisure there is still to be found, in many cases, the grit of a working life: salmon-netting on the Tamar, seaweed-dredging on the Fal, china clay and fertilizer, animal feed and roadstone, lobster-potting, trawling, oyster-dredging and boatbuilding. Were it not for this secret life, and for those few remaining wildernesses untouched by improvements and restoration, Cornwall would long since have been engulfed by inanity. The secret life, the dignity of undiscovered places, the thrill of the wilderness . . . to be preserved they need only to be left alone.

This book covers just those harbours on Cornwall's dramatically varied south coast – from the wild and vulnerable Lamorna Cove in the west to the rich and salty lushness of the Tamar Valley in the east. Given that harbours and estuaries and the lands around them can only really be explored by boat or on foot, it is thus from the waterborne and perambulant points of view only that each small discovery is made.

All of the places mentioned in the book may be found on the relevant sheets of the Ordnance Survey 1:25 000 maps, and many are included in the 1:50 000 range.

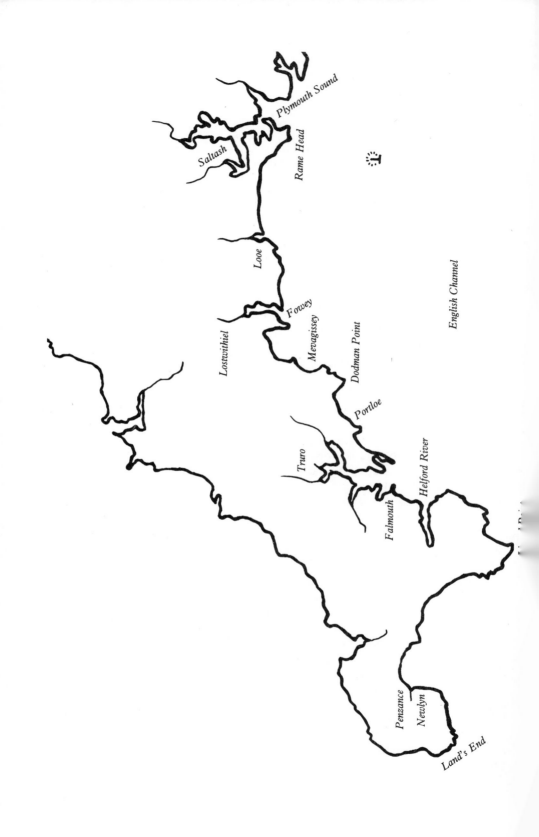

# Contents

# Introduction

My window, then, looks out from a small library upon a small harbour frequented by ships of all nations—British, Danish, Swedish, Norwegian, Russian, French, German, Italian, with now and then an American or a Greek—and upon a shore which I love because it is my native country. Of all views I reckon that of a harbour the most fascinating and the most easeful, for it combines perpetual change with perpetual repose. It amuses like a panorama and soothes like an opiate, and when you have realised this you will understand why so many thousands of men around this island appear to spend all their time in watching tidal water.

Arthur Quiller-Couch, 'Q', *From a Cornish Window* (1906)

*'There is just a lonely expanse of sea'*

# 1  Mount's Bay

The smoke from the cottages and trawler funnels is rising blue and straight; the brown sails of the fishing boats are still set, and chequer the forest of masts with rich notes of colour; a three-masted Russian schooner with a white hull, massive and rough hewn, is lying at the quayside; while an old hulk, once a broad-sparred brig, whose bluff bows have cut the water of every sea, slumbers in the centre of the harbour, to which its storm-worn, bulky presence lends a rare distinction.

> Newlyn on a still June evening—A. G. Folliott Stokes:
> *From Land's End to the Lizard* (1909)

## Lamorna Cove

THERE is only a stumpy little granite pier to give Lamorna any more right than the other lovely coves of Penwith (Penberth, Porthgwarra, Porthcurno—all tiny fishing ports in their own right) to be regarded as a harbour. Moreover it can only loosely be considered as part of Mount's Bay, the grandest bay in Cornwall, for it is not in the inner sanctum; the broken headland of Carn-du sees to that. When you stand on the pier looking out, there is nothing safe or familiar in the view; you cannot see the elegant sweep of the shore or the shadowy figure of St Michael's Mount in the distance. There is just a lonely expanse of sea, with the long smudge of the Lizard far away. Lamorna feels very isolated and exposed.

## THE HARBOUR

The short, thick pier owes its existence to the granite quarries which used to flourish here. First opened in 1849 under the ownership of the famous Freeman brothers, the Lamorna quarries needed a shipping point nearby for quick delivery of the huge blocks to Penzance. At first this was provided by a timber jetty built out into the cove by the mouth of the Lamorna stream. The stone pier was built in 1854, and incorporated an unusual feature in a limekiln (now a store) which produced lime to mortar the wall's granite. Lamorna should then have been an ideal site for an expanding granite industry and port, but the cove suffered badly from its exposure to heavy seas. There were many reports in the later 19th century of its unpopularity, and of ships having to put to sea two or three times during loading to avoid being wrecked. These troubles put the price of the granite up to a prohibitive level and it was not long before the pier was abandoned in favour of laborious road transport to Penzance.

The harbour continued to provide shelter for the occasional fishing boat, and a wooden crane was fixed on the wall for lowering boats into the water, but for much of the time there was only one fisherman working here, and the wall began to crumble away into the sea. When pleasure trips from Penzance to Lamorna, for cream teas in the cottage gardens, became fashionable in the 1920s, a landing stage was built on the opposite side of the cove to the tumbling harbour wall. During the Second World War the wooden crane was dismantled by the American forces in order to make things difficult for any invaders.

The pier's present trimness dates from the 1950s, when much of the cove was bought by Mr John Daniel. He had the end of the wall repaired, although not restored to its former length, and made the discovery among the fallen blocks of the old text stone which had been built into the original pier; this he had incorporated into the restored section:

> 'Except the Lord build the house,
> They labour in vain that build it.'

A slipway was also made for fishing boats, and Lamorna now has a surprisingly healthy mackerel fishery.

No modern intrusions can detract from the wildness of Lamorna Cove. The old quarry cottages may be neat and suburbanized and bear names such as 'Sunnyvale', and the cars may crowd boldly on to the waterfront, but this will always be a primitive place with its steep, braky hillsides heaving with granite outcrops, its untamed valley and the chaotic beach just a mass of vast boulders, and with the towering quarry dumps on the east of the cove poised, like waterfalls of stone, above the unsuspecting cottages. Lamorna Cove is a part of the strange, powerful landscape of

Penwith; the influence of the present century does not go very deep here, the 'lone majesty of untamed nature' (as J. Ayrton Paris called it in 1828) is still in control.

## UP PAST THE QUARRIES

From the cove, it is usual to walk out along the coastal path towards Carn-du in one direction or Carn Mellyn and Carn Barges in the other (the Cornish names mean Black Head, Yellow Head and Buzzard Head respectively). There is also a little used circular walk along the old quarry paths which encompasses much of the fascination of the Lamorna valley. Taking the coastal path towards Carn-du at first, up past the garage block (once one of the quarry smithies), turn left in front of the 'Sunnyvale' cottages on to a narrow footpath. This heads off up the valley, then curls around towards the sea again, climbing all the while. A short-cut straight up the hillside, still shown on the Ordnance Survey map, is now no longer passable.

This silent pathway used to be the main route from quarry to cove and was, according to Susie Mitchell in her *Recollections of Lamorna* (on sale in the cove shop), known as Chain Lane, for it was this way that the huge blocks were dragged with chains down to the pier. There is quite a temptation to become fanciful when walking alone up Chain Lane, and even if it is resisted the sudden emergence into the largest of the Lamorna quarries may prove to be your undoing. This is a lonely place with a strange hush—that emptiness of sound which is left behind after men and industry have moved away. Gorse fills the shells of the quarry buildings, and you can walk out on the turf-bound, and surprisingly secure, crests of the granite tips for a breathtaking view down into the cove.

The path then zig-zags back again and climbs towards the second of the quarries (the third is just beyond) and the heart of the fantastic landscape of stone tips, a hidden place overhanging the quilted valley. Here the path doubles back once more and begins its final ascent towards Kemyel Wartha.

This meagre path was the main way to Mousehole and Penzance, and thus the route taken by the stone-carrying wagons after sea shipment was abandoned and a steam-powered crane erected in the first quarry to lift the stone to the top of the valley. The most dangerous part of the journey came when the heavily laden wagons descended the long, steep Paul Hill into Newlyn. In the other direction came quarry supplies, including gunpowder which made for a dangerous journey in itself.

Lamorna granite continued to be quarried until about 1911. The stone from the three eastern quarries (the western one was a failure) was of high quality. Shipped from Penzance, it was used in building the breakwaters at Alderney and Portland, the Admiralty Pier at Dover, parts of Devonport Dockyard, the Bishop Rock, Wolf Rock and Longships lighthouses; and in London, the Bank of New Zealand at Moorgate, the Café Monico in Piccadilly, Lloyds Bank in Lombard Street and New Scotland Yard.

Lamorna granite even went to the Great Exhibition in 1851: a 24 foot 4 inch high obelisk weighing over 20 tons which was transported slowly and gingerly by wagon to Penzance. ('I wonder what became of it,' mused J. Harris Stone in 1912, 'for it was not an article to carry about in a waistcoat pocket.')

Where the quarry path reaches Kemyel Wartha, a signed footpath heads off to the left in the direction of the distant church of St Buryan, clear on the skyline. Further on, as the track makes its way across the tousled valley side, the horizon swells up into the old hills of Penwith: Chapel Carn Brea, Bartinney Downs, Caer Bran and Sancreed Beacon.

The path emerges on to the road just above Lamorna Mill, an ancient building formed with massive irregular stones, which until 1907 still used the old wooden gearing. Milling ceased altogether in 1919 and it is now an idyllically placed craft and plant shop. Just downhill there is another smaller mill almost buried in the riotous garden—a steamy paradise of giant rhubarb and rushing water, rampaging down towards the Lamorna stream in the valley bottom. Just before crossing this stream you will see a faint path on the left, the old quarry track from Lamorna village down to the cove. It leads through the secret heart of the Lamorna valley (wild mounds and stagnant green pools) beside the tumbling river until you reach Chain Lane again. 'This is a valley that must be taken slowly', wrote S. P. B. Mais in 1928, and every temptation to wander casually succumbed to.'

## THE ARTISTS

It was the beauty and the light in valley and cove, and the trout in the stream, that brought the artist Samuel John Birch to live here, up at Boleigh, towards the end of the last century. The presence of Birch, himself led to Cornwall by the presence of Stanhope Forbes and others in Newlyn, attracted other artists to settle in Lamorna and form something of a colony. It was Stanhope Forbes who suggested that he take the name 'Lamorna' to distinguish him from another Birch, painting in Newlyn at the time, and it was through Lamorna Birch and his friends that the name of this small valley became known far beyond the shores of Cornwall. After his marriage in 1902 Lamorna Birch moved into the old Coastguard's house Flagstaff Cottage, above the cove, and there he stayed, when others moved away, until his death in 1955. His daughter Lamorna Kerr, who as a child was painted by both Augustus John and Laura Knight, lives here still and has on permanent exhibition some of her father's works, as well as many glorious pictures of her own. Many of Lamorna Birch's paintings are fortunately still in the county, such as the wonderful 'Morning Fills the Bowl', a radiant portrayal of Lamorna Cove which can be seen in the County Museum in Truro. At Penlee House in Penzance, even closer to home, there is now a permanent exhibition of the paintings owned by the town, six of which including the unforgettable 'Kerris Quarry' are by Lamorna Birch.

Other artists who visited or settled in the area and became associated with the Lamorna Group included Ella and Charles Napier who lived at Trewoofe, Eleanor and Robert Hughes at Chyangwheal near Boleigh, and Laura and Harold Knight at Oakhill Cottages near Trewoofe.

The charismatic Alfred (A. J.) Munnings, who went on to achieve great fame and success, spent many years in Lamorna. He lived at first at the Wink, Lamorna's inn, and had a studio at the mill, and then moved to Cliff House after his marriage to Florence in 1912. Two years later she committed suicide by taking cyanide; he rarely spoke of her again. The Wink, which is still going strong and full of atmosphere, was run in those days by a Mr Jory, quite a character by all accounts; his wife, to whom he never spoke, ran the rival Temperance Hotel just up the hill. This hotel, which began life as the quarry manager's house (with a chapel attached for the workers, of which the bell tower can still be seen), is now the highly acclaimed Lamorna Cove Hotel. Among the many artists who used to stay at the Temperance was Augustus John, whose wife used to cause quite a stir by walking out on Sundays not wearing a hat. It was the Wink, however, which was the Lamorna artists' local; Robert Hughes had a regular daily routine which involved making for the Wink every lunchtime, after a morning's painting, to smoke his pipe and play a few hands of euchre. The familiar scene inside the pub was painted by both Munnings and Harold Knight, and the atmosphere captured by Father Walke in the wonderful story of Joe Ladner and the Lord which he tells in his autobiography *Twenty Years at St Hilary*. Bernard Walke was the parish priest of St Hilary, on the far side of Mount's Bay, from 1912 to 1936, and his church is gloriously decorated with the work of many of his Lamorna and Newlyn friends. Despite the destruction of the granite altars and some works of art in the church in 1932, by those opposed to Father Walke's Anglo-Catholicism, many beautiful things survived. It is extraordinarily exciting to visit this church and see the unassuming paintings on the choir stalls by Harold Knight, Dod and Ernest Procter, Gladys Hynes, Norman and Althea Garstin, Harold Harvey and Annie Walke (Bernard's wife); the dramatic crucifix by Phyllis Yglesias (who later started the Mousehole Wild Bird Hospital); and the uncannily skilful pictures by the ten-year-old Joan Manning-Saunders depicting the childhood of Christ.

The artistic tradition endures in Lamorna, with potters, writers, painters and artisans scattered among the trees; Lamorna Kerr paints on in Flagstaff Cottage, a vivid link with the past, while a new generation of artists is working in her father's first studio, the tin-roofed building in a lush valley garden a little way up the lane.

## Mousehole

'Picturesque and odiferous is Mousehole', wrote J. Harris Stone in 1912, and although less odiferous these days, since most of the Mount's Bay catches are landed at Newlyn, it is still remarkably picturesque and unspoilt and, to my mind, the fairest of all Cornish harbours.

*'Fairest of all Cornish harbours'*

## THE HARBOUR

Mousehole was once the most important fishing port in Mount's Bay. A market was granted here, proof of its prominence, as early as 1266, whereas Penzance had to wait until 1332; and when the Duchy of Cornwall was created in 1337, Mousehole paid an annual rent of £5 as compared with the 12 shillings paid by Penzance. Even as late as the 1530s, John Leland (the King's Antiquary, who travelled throughout the country on a fact-finding mission) could still write that 'Newlin is an Hamlet to Mousehole'. He also mentioned Porthennis, Mousehole's Cornish name which means 'the harbour of the island', a reference to St Clement's Isle which still, in Leland's time, had 'a Chapel of St Clementes', the patron saint of ships. There is nothing on the island now but a stone pillar set up as a mark of ownership in 1890, and it is hard to imagine a more exposed and perilous site for a chapel than this low rambling rock ('like a sprawling lion' Douglas Tregenza calls it in *Departed Days—Mousehole Remembered*).

Mousehole was possibly the first Cornish port to be given an artificial pier, because of both its importance and its particularly exposed position. The old pier was built after 1389, when land was granted to build a quay for men and boats, and is now part of the longer South or Great Quay. It was extended in the early 18th century and again in the last century, but the old part with its massive irregular blocks is still easy to pick out. The new northern pier was built in the late 1860s. Although Mousehole's

12

importance waned from the 16th century onwards with the rise of Penzance and Newlyn, there was something of a revival in the mackerel fishery in the last century: in 1849, for instance, there were about 430 men employed in fishing alone, with a further 420 or so men and women working in the allied trades such as packing, curing and cooperage.

If fishing has declined since that high point, the courage and seamanship of Mousehole men have not. One famous tale concerns the wreck of the Thames sailing barge *Baltic* which went ashore on St Clement's Isle one dark night in November 1907. The Coastguards were alerted when her crew set fire to a paraffin soaked mattress, and six Mousehole fishermen, not waiting for the lifeboat, set out for the island in their crabber, having first had to hoist her over the wooden baulks which block the harbour entrance during storms. In rough seas and among treacherous reefs it took them five attempts to make a landing, but they eventually managed to rescue the three men and two women from the *Baltic* and to land them, with great difficulty, on the South Quay, the women being hauled up by ropes tied under their arms. This dedication and skill helps to explain why Mousehole men have for so long formed the crews of the Penlee lifeboat.

For thousands of people in this country and abroad the name Mousehole speaks of one thing—the tragedy of December 19, 1981 when eight Mousehole men, the entire crew of the Penlee lifeboat *Solomon Browne*, were drowned in trying to save the lives of those on the coaster *Union Star*. In mountainous seas just off Tater-du, beyond Lamorna Cove, lifeboat and coaster were overwhelmed and all were lost. Ordinary people of completely different backgrounds, with no knowledge of or connection with the sea, can remember quite clearly what they were doing that stormy night, or the next day when they heard the news, so deeply and universally was the tragedy felt. How a small community such as this can ever recover it is hard to imagine, but one thing has not changed: there are still Mousehole men in the crew of the new Penlee lifeboat, which is kept now in the harbour at Newlyn.

## THE VILLAGE

The new pier and many of the houses in Mousehole are built of the dense, fine-grained Lamorna granite which gives the place a look of solidity. The oldest part of the village is clustered around The Wharf, in the lee of the old pier. Just back from the harbour front here are Mousehole's two oldest houses, once inns called the Keigwin Arms and the Standard. These were the only buildings to survive what must be one of the strangest events in our island history: the Spanish invasion of Cornwall. July 23, 1995 will mark the 400th anniversary of the arrival of four Spanish galleons in Mount's Bay, seven years after the Armada, and the landing of 200 troops who subsequently set fire to Mousehole, Paul, Newlyn and Penzance. Soon after the event Richard Carew wrote an account of it in his celebrated *Survey of Cornwall*, which began:

'The 23rd of July, 1595, soon after the sun was risen and had chased a fog which before kept the sea out of sight, four galleys of the enemy presented themselves upon the coast over-against Mousehole, and there in a fair bay landed about 200 men, pikes and shot, who forthwith sent their forlorn hope, consisting of their basest people, unto the straggled houses of the country about half a mile compass or more, by whom were burned not only the houses they went by but also the parish church of Paul, the force of the fire being such as it utterly ruined all the great stone pillars thereof. Others of them in that time burned that fisher town Mousehole, the rest marched as a guard for defence of these firers.' He goes on to describe the half-hearted attempts at defence, the burning of Newlyn and Penzance, and the Spaniards' eventual departure after a show of strength by Sir Francis Godolphin and some reinforcements from Plymouth. If it all seems too fantastic to be true, there are still some reminders of the invasion to be seen, such as the scorched stone arch in Paul church and parish register entries that include 'Jenken Keigwin of Mousehole, being killed by the Spaniards, was buried ye 24 of Julii 1595'.

The Keigwin and the Standard, which at that time formed the manor house of the Keigwin family, survived the burning and became two of Mousehole's six pubs, of which only one has survived the decline of the fishing industry. The Ship Inn, which bears a slate tablet on its wall to commemorate the landlord Charles Greenhaugh who went down with the *Solomon Browne*, was a favourite haunt of Dylan Thomas when he lived here in the 1930s. He described Mousehole as 'the loveliest village in England', which would have been a generous compliment if only he had said 'Britain'.

## TO THE CAVE

A little way to the south of the village there is a tall, mournful cave draped in ferns, known as the Cave or the Mousehole, which in the Victorian age and later when natural wonders could still be tourist attractions, was quite a popular draw. To reach it you first have to climb a little way up the achingly steep Raginnis Hill ('Raginnis-is-good-for-you Hill', as Dylan Thomas used to call it), which is home to the famous wild bird hospital started by the Yglesias sisters. The view from Raginnis Hill is particularly fine: the far sweep of Mount's Bay and then the curve of Mousehole below; the roofs of houses old and new and the stones of the harbour walls tinged yellow with salty lichen as though the whole village had been scattered with pollen. The path to the Cave heads off to the left by the postbox, before you reach the wild bird hospital, and leads you out to the cliffs, on to a grassy level by the strange formations of Merlyn Rock. This level is known as the Battery (cannon were erected here after the Spanish raid) and was once a favourite resting place for visitors to the Cave. One enterprising villager set up a soft drinks stall here, while others acted as guides and raconteurs. Access to the Cave, just around the corner, was easier in those days; there used to be railings attached to the rocks all the way down, but now there are just two iron handholds.

The low headland beyond the Cave is called Point Spaniard and is where the invading force is supposed to have landed. There is another version, however, which has the Spaniards coming ashore on Merlyn Rock, thus fulfilling an ancient Cornish prophecy: 'Aga syth tyer, war an meyne Merlyn,/Ara neb syth Leskey Paul, Penzance, hag Newlyn', meaning 'There shall land on the stone of Merlyn,/Those who shall burn Paul, Penzance and Newlyn'. The fear engendered among the locals by the prophecy coming true is used to explain their state of panic and lack of resistance. Carew is the first writer to record the prophecy; did he, being patriotic, invent it to save Cornish pride, or was it the shamefaced locals who swiftly made it up, or is it really the truth? Mind you, neither Merlyn Rock nor Point Spaniard is particularly inviting as a landing place—perhaps neither version is true.

## UP TO PAUL

The road from Mousehole up to the friendly little churchtown of Paul is known as the Lane. Inside the church, which is unexpectedly large and barn-like with a very tall tower (an age-old seamark, it alone survived the burning), you will find one of the many memorials to the crew of the *Solomon Browne* (there are others in Mousehole's Wesleyan Chapel, for instance). This simple and striking memorial is a vast sea-smoothed granite boulder, weighing a ton, which was chosen from the beach at Lamorna, just around the corner from the cliffs at Tater-du and the scene of the tragedy.

## Newlyn

### THE HARBOUR

Newlyn harbour is a pretty exciting place to be at any time of day and on any day of the week; it is even exciting to read about it from miles away, as you can every week in *The Cornishman* newspaper in a fascinating maritime gossip column which discusses the movements in and out of Penzance and Newlyn harbours.

Any working port is an exhilarating place, but Newlyn is particularly so, perhaps because the harbour is so large and thriving, and there are so many fishing boats of all sizes here (an average of 120 commercial fishing vessels use the harbour); and because there is a pride in the knowledge that it is one of the top three or four fishing ports, in terms of catch value, in the country. In the year ending March 1986, for instance, the value of fish landed was over £9½ million, a massive increase of £2 million on the 1985 figures. The harbour is also still involved in other trade, particularly the export of roadstone from the quarry at Penlee Point. This stone is loaded from conveyors on the South Quay and the tonnage handled is growing; in the year 1985/6 it reached 106,000 (30,000 up on the year before), of which roughly a third was shipped to places outside the UK.

*'An exciting place to be at any time of day'*

Newlyn owes its prosperity partly to the extensive and farsighted harbour works carried out between 1866 and 1888 which provided the port with magnificent berthing facilities at all stages of the tide and in all weathers. It is extraordinary to compare this huge 43 acre harbour (which had further improvements in 1959, 1980 and 1983 with more in the pipeline) with the first tiny wall of the medieval port which lies deep in the belly of the grand new harbour, its huge old stones lichen-yellow and tufty with grass.

Throughout the 19th century Newlyn had one of the most successful of Cornish fisheries, partly through its adaptability in terms of methods and skills, and its promptness in developing a large drift-netting fishery well in advance of the others; and by the end of the century it was one of the top mackerel ports in Britain. This does not mean, however, that there has been a steady improvement in Newlyn's fortunes over the last 200 years: far from it. Fishing will always be an unreliable business, and Newlyn's switchback fortunes were aggravated in the late 19th century by the influx of fishermen from the East Coast ports, who, with little respect for the strong Christian principles of the Cornish fishermen, continued to fish right through the Sabbath. Using steam drifters after 1893, and fishing Saturday and Sunday nights, they flooded the markets so that by the time the Mount's Bay boats sold their catches on the Tuesday morning the prices were disastrously low. On a Monday in May 1896, a little before

16

seven in the morning, a group of nearly a thousand Newlyn and Mousehole fishermen and women made their way towards the harbour and the twelve East Country boats which had so far returned from the fishing grounds. Twenty or thirty men boarded one boat after another along the line, forced the crews ashore and threw all the mackerel into the harbour. Local men then captured three more boats which had been hovering outside the harbour, brought them in and dumped their catches too. Chains were then slung across the harbour entrance, and in Mousehole and Porthleven the wooden baulks were lowered into place, to keep out the rest of the East Country fleet. The atmosphere grew uglier as the day wore on; pubs were closed and bands of local men armed with barrel staves chased the Lowestoft and Yarmouth captains along the quays, baying 'Drown them! Drown them!' Eventually the Newlyn police chief had to call in the Army to restore the peace, and a gunboat and two torpedo boats, with armed parties on board, were sent down from Devonport. Cornishmen did not profit from the Newlyn Riots: in the following weeks the East Countrymen continued to fish on the Sabbath, and found a sympathetic reception at Penzance (ever keen to score points off Newlyn) where quayside improvements were swiftly undertaken at the request of the East Coast fish buyers and shipowners.

## THE NEWLYN SCHOOL

Why it is that Newlyn should have become such a magnet for artists in the 1880s and 1890s, and such an inspiration and focus for one of the great movements in English art, it is hard to imagine nowadays. Even Stanhope Forbes, who is today considered the father of the school, could not fully explain the curious magnetism of the place: 'What lodestone of artistic metal the place contains I know not, but its effects were strongly felt in the studios of Paris and Antwerp particularly, by a number of young English painters studying there who just about then, by some common impulse, seemed drawn towards this corner of their native land.'

Walter Langley, Edwin Harris, Ralph Todd, Leghe Suthers, Fred Hall, Frank Bramley, T. C. Gotch and Percy Craft had all arrived in Newlyn before Forbes, who came in 1884. By the late 1880s most of those artists principally associated with the Newlyn School had settled in the village, and some had already left. The binding principle of this early group was a passionate belief in the importance of painting in the open air. Accustomed as we are nowadays to the sight of easels dotted about at beauty spots, especially along the quays of Cornish harbours, it is not easy to appreciate just how revolutionary an idea this was at the time: to the English establishment it all seemed rather eccentric and Continental.

Stanhope Forbes' cool, clear 'Fish Sale on a Cornish Beach', which he painted while '. . . fighting with the east wind before a large canvas on the cold and sloppy beach between Newlyn and Penzance', first drew national attention to what was going on in Newlyn. It hangs today in Plymouth's City Art Gallery.

17

Stanhope Forbes and his wife Elizabeth (née Armstrong) stayed on when many of the others left, built a house at the top of Paul Hill (Higher Faugan, now a hotel) and founded a school of painting which attracted a whole new generation of artists down here, many of whom eventually settled in Lamorna.

In recent years, the artists of the Newlyn School and their successors in Newlyn and Lamorna have been enjoying a dramatic revival of interest. There have been two major exhibitions mounted by the Newlyn Orion Gallery in 1979 and 1985 (both of which had excellent catalogues by Caroline Fox), a television film about the artists, and sales held in London have attracted international attention.

## THE TOWN

Newlyn has changed a great deal since those days of picturesque squalor and poverty. Inevitably, however, not all the changes have been for the better. As early as 1900, Stanhope Forbes was driven to launch a stirring attack upon modern building in his address to the Royal Cornwall Polytechnic Society in which he warned that: 'Age and wear will alike be powerless to impart charm or interest to the tawdry workmanship which so often today replaces the fine old simple taste of our forefathers.'

Significantly, it was not just the artists who were concerned about the changes in Newlyn. In 1937 it was decided that the old harbour wall, much of Fore Street and many of the old properties on the hill behind were to be demolished. Local feeling was so strongly against the plans that a group of fishermen sailed all the way up to Westminster in the 50 foot long-liner *Rosebud* and presented a petition to Sir Kingsley Wood, the Minister of Housing. The planned developments never took place; the charms of Newlyn today owe their survival either to the men of the *Rosebud,* or to the outbreak of war, or perhaps to both.

Everywhere you go in Newlyn you are reminded of the importance of fish. Down by the harbour the long fish market dominates, wet and echoing after the hubbub of the early morning sale, and behind it lurks the old ice factory. Warehouses all over the town are filled with fish and shellfish, and the strong and prosperous smell leaps out at you as you pass by.

There are many reminders of Newlyn's fishing past as well. Many of the houses have extra-wide doorways to allow for the passage of hogsheads of fish, dating from the time when all fishermen had small cellars in their cottages for the salting and pressing of pilchards for the family: those at the bottom of Church Street, for example.

Even in St Peter's Church, a little way up the Coombe, you will find reminders that this is a fishing congregation, like the two small and beautiful stained glass windows depicting Jesus with the fishermen:

'He arose and rebuked the winds and the sea and there was great calm.'

'Cast the net on the right side of the ship and ye shall find.'

The church is relatively modern (1865), because Newlyn used to be divided between the parishes of Paul and Madron, and is rather splendid with its blue and white painted wooden ceiling like a French barn; the chancel lit up brightly, the rest of the church dark and cool.

Just down from the church there is a dazzling fairytale building, now the Meadery, which used to be Newlyn's Gaiety Cinema. It opened in about 1923 and was popular with all Newlyn people including the artists, some of whom, for instance Harold Harvey and Cedric Norris, featured it in their paintings. A little way along New Road towards Penzance is the Passmore Edwards Art Gallery, the Newlyn Orion, headquarters since 1895 of the Newlyn Society of Artists. Exhibitions are still regularly mounted here and the Society, along with the Penwith Society of Artists in St Ives, does much to encourage the large number of artists still working in Penwith.

The Newlyn School artists tended, in general, to live and work in a little knot of lanes and alleyways above Fore Street; around North Corner, Trewarveneth Street, Gwavas Road, Boase Street and Church Street. Dylan Thomas also lived on this side of Newlyn for a while after his marriage to Caitlin Macnamara in Penzance on July 11, 1937. On August 6 he wrote in a letter to Pamela Hansford Johnson that he was 'a long way from everywhere, in a high huge haystack of a studio over the harbour . . . drinking scaly beer in the pubs near the fish market'. Much has changed, but you can still, on occasions, glimpse something of the Newlyn which so captivated the first artists; you might glance down an alley or through an archway and find a small scrubbed courtyard with tubs of flowers and grass-grown cobbles and the demure white backs of cottages—a place of accidental charm. Halfway up Trewarveneth Street there is a tiny alley-way on the left called, rather incongruously Rue des Beaux Arts. This previously nameless passage was 'a little nest of artists' studios' according to J. Harris Stone, and it was MacIver Grierson, Fred Evans and Edwin Harris who first, with gentle irony, gave it the name which has since become official. In one of the cottages here Frank Bramley painted his 'Hopeless Dawn'. This mournful painting of two women waiting, slumped in despair in the cool dawn light, by the window of a cottage which overlooks the bay, made a great impression on the artistic establishment of the day, and continues to have a powerful appeal. It now hangs in the Tate Gallery.

Opposite the Rue des Beaux Arts is the old Infants' School, which was an artist's studio before becoming a school in 1901; the lane at the back of it led to The Meadow, a piece of untamed land which from about 1888 onwards began to sprout purpose-built glass studios to cater for the artists. 'The Meadow' became the social and cultural centre of the colony and the artists used to hold picnics here, and private views until the Passmore Edwards Gallery was built in 1895. Despite the rapid development of Newlyn, there is still some clear ground here, below 'Belle Vue' and above the old school, with a few apple trees and macrocarpas and a magnificent view out over Mount's Bay.

## Penzance

Penzance has style; it is hard to miss it. Although the town has the economic problems of being at the end of the line, a depressingly high unemployment rate, and areas of dilapidation and decay, what comes through loud and clear is the colour in the streets and an air of excitement and innovation. Local planners, promoters, politicians and theorists are eager to highlight the disadvantages of Cornwall's inaccessibility, and much effort is directed to improving communications with the outside world, but there are also positive effects, not the least of which is the genuine originality fostered by remoteness in places like Penzance.

### THE HARBOUR

Things are about to change around Penzance harbour; in ten years' time, if the plans agreed in October 1986 are stuck to, the whole harbour area will be a very different place indeed. There will be superstores, shopping complexes, landscaping, a huge leisure centre and a rerouted harbour road: the jangle of tourism and commerce will have replaced the dignified, if shabby, echoes of a great trading port. What is wrong with Penzance harbour now is not the dilapidation of its quayside buildings but the huge car park which has swallowed up half of the basin, and the faceless, tasteless grey monstrosity that is Tesco's. If the *spirit* of the new development is wrong, is not maritime, then no amount of costly 'heritage' preservation will save the harbour.

Penzance probably had its first stone pier in the 15th century; before this, shelter for boats would have come from the small rocky headland to the south of the harbour which, together with the chapel which once stood there, gave the town its name (pen sans is Cornish for the 'holy headland'). In the early medieval period both Penzance and Newlyn were inferior to Mousehole, but by the time of the harbour charter of 1512 things were beginning to pick up, and a century later, when Penzance was incorporated as a borough, the town was quite prosperous although there was still serious competition from the ancient market town of Marazion with its harbour on the Mount. Penzance's Harbour Charter of 1512, which bears the signature of King Henry VIII, grants to the people of Penzance 'alle manner of profits' from the 'ankerage kylage and bussellage of every shippe that shall herafter fortune to arryve and resorte at and to our seid towne or kaye'. The harbour at this time consisted of what is now the quay at the back wall of the floating dock which has the disused china clay warehouse running along it, and a straight stretch of harbour wall on the site of the South Pier.

In 1663 Charles II made Penzance a coinage town for the stannary of Penwith which, under regulations laid down by King John, meant that tin was weighed and assayed here twice a year for the purpose of taxation. The creation of this new coinage town marked a westward movement of the centre of tin mining (the old coinage towns of Bodmin and Lostwithiel were abolished at the same time), and it brought prosperity and expansion to both the town and the harbour. The old pier was rebuilt in the 18th century, and from then on until the end of the last century there were regular improvements being made to the harbour. In May 1810, for instance, local shipbuilder John Mathews announced that he had completed 'a safe and very commodious Dry Dock, capable of receiving ships or vessels from One Hundred to Five Hundred tons burthen'. It was, according to the *West Briton*, 'considered by all the nautical men who have seen it, to be the first dry dock in the West of England'. Later, the Mathews family had two more built, one of which was at the foot of New Town Lane near the gasworks.

In August 1858 one of the harbour's most enduring functions began with the launching of the first steamer service to the Isles of Scilly. The *Scotia* sailed three times a week there and back, and in December was joined by another steamer, the *Little Western*. A trip to Scilly today on the *Scillonian* is still one of life's great excitements; the helicopter service, although quick, comfortable and not at all sick-making, will never command such affection. There even exists a club made up of the passengers on one particular crossing when every single person on board went down with seasickness.

During the 19th century trade was varied and vigorous; nearly half of Cornwall's tin was shipped from Penzance and there was vice-consular representation in the town for Turkey, Portugal, Spain, France, Holland, Oldenburg, Prussia, Mecklenburg, Hanover, Denmark, Norway and Sweden. The most extensive changes to the actual layout of the harbour came in the 1870s and 1880s with the extension to the Northern Pier, the creation of the floating dock and the building of the harbour road. The three Mathews dry docks were all put out of action by the new works—the New Town Lane one was cut off from the harbour by the road, the road also blocked the entrance to another, and the Ross Swing Bridge was built on the site of the third—so a new one was built in 1880 with its entrance off the swinging berth to which access was provided by the Ross Bridge. This dry dock was bought in 1904 by N. Holman & Sons, a firm of founders, engineers and ship repairers which had started back in 1834 with the building of the St Just foundry. Holmans' Penzance foundry, which opened five years later, was located on the side of Mathews' shipyard at the foot of New Town Lane, and it was here that the railings along the Terrace in Market Jew Street were fashioned by hand in 1873. Holmans are still at work in the dry dock, and they have built up a worldwide reputation for fine and efficient craftsmanship. This historic enterprise, with its huge green corrugated sheds and bold white lettering, is the best thing about the harbour and should be the pride of Penzance as a whole.

## THE TOWN

The street plan of medieval Penzance was still much the same in 1780 when the Rev. John Swete described it as 'consisting of one very long street leading from west to east, and another dividing itself from this at the market place in the middle of the town, which conducts to the quay'; in other words, Chyandour Cliff through Market Jew Street and Alverton Street to Alverton Road, and Chapel Street and Quay Street (of these, Quay Street is supposed to be the oldest). The original complex at the market place of the market house and guildhall was demolished in 1838 and replaced by the present splendid granite market house, at the western end of which is a large statue of Sir Humphry Davy with a Lamorna granite base. The statue might be a little dirty, but it is still clear to see that Davy was a handsome and imposing man. Penzance born and bred, he was one of the greatest chemists this country has ever produced. (A. L. Rowse has called him '*the* Cornishman of genius *par excellence*'), and is today remembered chiefly for his vital invention of the miner's safety lamp. He was also, in true Renaissance spirit, a considerable poet who was much admired by Coleridge.

Running from the market house down towards the station is Market Jew Street, famous for its raised pavement which makes shopping in Penzance such a pleasure. There is still the overriding atmosphere of a market town here, setting it apart from all the other Cornish ports, because much of its historical importance came from its position as a market for tin, cloth and agricultural produce serving the whole of West Cornwall. It is also a town of compatible contrasts; in Causewayhead, for instance, picture framers, wholefood shops and outposts of alternative culture rub shoulders with ironmongers, shoeshops and grocers, while just around the corner in Bread Street (parallel to Market Jew Street) there is a real treat for anyone who likes big, solid 19th century warehouses: a whole wonderful streetful of them.

It is generally accepted that nothing much remains of the pre-Spanish Invasion Penzance, but smoke-blackened granite is discovered from time to time under layers of plaster, hardboard and paint suggesting that a particular piece of a specific building *might* date from that time. Scorched stone has recently been uncovered in the Union Hotel in Chapel Street, a building which now has an elegant Georgian facade but which, the proprietor believes, was a manor house in the late 16th century when Penzance was set on fire. The hotel has other interesting aspects. Its Nelson Bar is so called because the news of the death of Nelson and the victory of Trafalgar was announced for the first time in Britain from the minstrels' gallery in the hotel's Assembly Room, now the ballroom. In Georgian and Victorian times the hotel was the centre of society and entertainment in Penzance, and there is a fascinating reminder of those days in the survival of a late 18th century theatre at the rear of the building. In its heyday, the greatest actors in the country, like Edmund Keene and Henry Irving, appeared on stage at this, the second oldest theatre in Britain. At the time of writing, the hotel's owner is hoping to be able to restore and reopen the theatre in time for the 200th anniversary of its first performance in 1787.

Further down Chapel Street is St Mary's Church, a dominating structure for miles around, and particularly from the sea and the harbour. The church was built in 1834 on the site of the medieval chapel of St Mary's, and Folliott-Stokes described the church in 1909 as 'a modern structure that, but for the tower, might easily be mistaken for a railway station'. This is not such an insult today, in an age when stations are often much admired, some even inspiring nothing short of worship. Seen from the harbour, the church does look faintly ridiculous, like an overweight cuckoo squatting in a crowded nest, but it has the Victorian grandeur and certainty of the best stations—like York—to save it. St Mary's suffered a disastrous fire in March 1985 which has entailed a massive programme of rebuilding and restoration.

The permanent exhibition of the town's paintings in Penlee House, in Penlee Park, has already been mentioned because of its six Lamorna Birch pictures. Also on display are some of the best known Newlyn School works, like Percy Craft's 'Tucking a School of Pilchards', Norman Garstin's 'The Rain it Raineth', and several paintings by both Stanhope and Elizabeth Forbes. It is a fascinating collection which should not be missed.

Not far from Penlee Park you will find the Morrab Gardens; a little pocket of nostalgia and elegance with palm trees, a fountain, a bandstand and a fine library, wonderful bursts of colour from the flowerbeds, ornamental lilyponds and giant rhubarb plants. Whole areas of the town, like the Morrab Gardens, the Promenade and the Esplanade, are still steeped in the enchanting potion of genteel seaside town and fashionable watering-place that was Penzance in the last century. The seafront between Penzance and Newlyn, now taken up with the Promenade, the Esplanade and New Road, was once a place of industry rather than leisure. In 1909 an exasperated Folliott-Stokes found 'two hideous factories with three tall chimneys', one of which was undoubtedly Thomas Bodilly's massive steam-powered Laregan Flour Mill which stood from 1874 until the 1920s on the site now occupied by the bus depot. Some 120 years before his visit, Folliott-Stokes would have had even more to complain about as a successful tin mine then operated here. The Wherry was perhaps the most spectacular mine in Cornwall, the main shaft being sunk on the Wherry Reef (which is covered by 19 feet of water at high spring tides) and topped by a 20 foot high wooden turret. The shaft was too narrow for a ladder so the men were lowered and raised by a rope tied around their thighs; four men had to bail water using the windlass for two hours at the beginning of each shift; and the ore was ferried ashore by rowing boat. In 1798 an American ship broke loose from her moorings in Newlyn harbour during a storm and crashed into the tower, demolishing the machinery and flooding the mine. This was the end of the Wherry Mine; there was a brief spurt of activity when a new company was formed in 1836, but little came of it.

## St Michael's Mount

The Mount has surely inspired more poetry, more paintings and more purple passages than any other place in the county. It is Cornwall's darling—and why not? This is an extraordinary place for which familiarity breeds no contempt: the same thrill of that first sight is there every time. Like the perfect lover it has an unfailing power to surprise and delight with all its many changeful moods:

> Sometimes aloof from a phantasmal coast
> Thou gloomest in the fog, a sheeted ghost;
> Sometimes the morning's rose
> Quivers and glows,
> Or westering sunlight's vision of desire
> Sets thee afire,
> While lazily the boats around thy quay
> Sway to the seabirds and the lapping sea.
> (from A. L. Salmon's 'St Michael's Mount')

Milton wrote of it 'Great vision of the guarded Mount', and Turner painted it, with wonderful exaggeration; but not everyone has been so moved: 'To speak the truth of this so much talked of famous mount: it is lofty, rocky, inaccessible, impregnable, not to be taken, or kept, not worth the taking or keeping; it is a barren stony little wen or wart . . . .'. These are the words of the inimitable John Taylor, a man of many bizarre talents who visited Cornwall in 1649. Apart from Wilkie Collins's *Rambles Beyond Railways* written 200 years later, no account of a tour of Cornwall has ever come close to Taylor's *Wandering to see the Wonders of the West* (we will encounter it again at Mevagissey).

The Mount has been in the hands of the National Trust since 1954, although it is still the home of the St Aubyn family as it has been since 1659. Today the castle alone is the Trust's fifth most visited property; 165,000 people climbed the Pilgrims' Steps last year, while approximately twice as many just visit the village and harbour. This makes an average of nearly half a million modern-day pilgrims a year taking the Mount's ferries, or toiling across the causeway in the steps of their medieval predecessors (many of whom would have travelled for weeks or months to visit St Michael's Chair and to glimpse the jawbone of St Appolonia of Alexandria, the patron saint of toothache).

### THE HARBOUR AND VILLAGE

In approaching the Mount there is a curious feeling of going abroad, for there is something exotic and foreign about the setting of the castle and the subtropical plants and trees, but the harbour is solidly Cornish and familiar (although perhaps a little too clean). There is still a good island community here, and most of the people who run the Mount so smoothly, and seemingly with such ease despite the huge numbers of visitors, live here in the village.

*'. . . something exotic and foreign about the setting of the castle . . . but the harbour is solidly Cornish'*

The modern history of the harbour begins in the early 15th century with the construction of a stone jetty and the causeway, to give shelter for 200 vessels of around 80 tons each. There must have been some sort of breakwater, whether natural or man-made, in the Iron Age, when the Mount was probably a vital port on the old cross-Cornwall route from the Hayle estuary to Mount's Bay. It is also very possible that the Mount was the important 'Ictis' referred to in the writings of Pliny the Elder and Diodorus Siculus, both of whom based their accounts on works dating back to the 4th century BC which have since been lost. Diodorus's account, which is the longer, describes in detail the winning of tin in 'Belerium' (Penwith) and goes on to say:

'Then they work the tin into pieces the size of knuckle-bones and convey it to an island which lies off Britain and is called Ictis; for at the time of ebb-tide the space between this island and the mainland becomes dry and they can take the tin in large quantities over to the island on their wagons . . . On the island of Ictis the merchants purchase the tin of the natives and carry it from there across the Strait of Galatia or Gaul; and finally, making their way on foot through Gaul for some thirty days, they bring their wares on horseback to the mount of the river Rhone.'

Expert opinion has always been divided, and other places have been suggested for Ictis, but as Maxwell pointed out in his article in the *Journal* of the Royal Institution of Cornwall (1972), there are no valid objections to the Mount, and there is some positive evidence. The Mount is on the shortest possible trade route to Marseilles (via the Garonne River and the Carcassone gate), it was very near the tin-producing area, and it is still an island at high tide and part of the mainland at low tide.

Although there were fish cellars and nine houses on the Mount in 1481, and 'a Peere for Bootes and Shippes' and 'certen Howses with Shoppes for

Fyschermen' in Leland's day 60 years later, by 1700 there was only one inhabited cottage and much decay and depression. The settlement owed its survival to the then proprietor of the Mount, Sir John St Aubyn, who rebuilt the harbour in 1727 to promote tin exports and fishing. In 1811 there were 53 houses in four streets, and by 1873 the village had schools, pubs, a Wesleyan chapel, shop, bakery and Customs house, and a population of about 300. The new harbour was capable of taking 500-ton vessels, and had a thriving import trade in Scandinavian timber, coal and iron, and continued to export tin and copper ore for much of the century.

The copper trade picked up substantially after the rival port of Hayle began to have problems in the 1830s with a sand bar, but there were risks at the Mount too, just as must have troubled the Iron Age tin traders, as illustrated by this *West Briton* report of a wagon heavily laden with copper ore trying to cross to the Mount before the tide was fully out.

'The wagon had not gone far before the horses were obliged to swim, and the poor affrighted animals turned into still deeper water. Assistance was speedily at hand, and several boats put off and arrived just in time to save the life of a lad who had been riding the fore horse, which was unfortunately drowned. With the utmost difficulty, the other horses were set at liberty and towed to land. Several other wagons were following, but stopped in time to avoid danger.'

The harbour had achieved its present form by 1824 when the reconstruction and enlargements undertaken by a later Sir John St Aubyn were completed. Competition from Penzance harbour, which had a railway link after 1852, eventually put an end to the Mount's trading life and many of the old cottages were demolished. Improvements made since the National Trust took over have included the recent conversion of the old sail loft and carpenter's shop into a restaurant, using, with admirable enterprise, granite salvaged from the disused railway platforms at St Columb station.

## THE CASTLE

Today the building is cleverly divided between private and public areas, so that you do not feel you are missing anything, and yet when you are standing on the South Terrace admiring the view there are five floors of the St Aubyns' private quarters dropping away precipitously, like a Tibetan monastery, beneath you.

Highlights of the tour include the fascinating tidal clock in Sir John's Room, the massive 1748 map by Thomas Martyn outside the museum (the best early map of Cornwall), and the series of recent paintings by the Cornish artist John Miller from Sancreed near Penzance, hung in the passage beyond the museum.

The most famous room in the castle is the Chevy Chase room which takes its name from the 17th century plaster frieze depicting hunting scenes. This room and the library next door are in the oldest part of the building, the main remnant of the monastery built on the Mount in 1135 by Bernard le Bec. He was the Abbot of Mont St Michel in Normandy, and this new Benedictine Priory was built as a cell or dependency of the senior abbey. The Chevy Chase room was the monastic refectory; its roof is 15th century and its walls may well be 300 years older. After the monastery was dissolved under Henry VIII the Crown appointed Governors to oversee the garrison which had existed here since the 12th century, and then sold it off into private hands not long afterwards. The Royalist Bassett family held the Mount during the Civil War, and when it was finally captured in April 1646 the castle was found to contain 30 guns, 100 barrels of gunpowder, 500 muskets and 100 pikes. After the war the Parliamentarian Colonel John St Aubyn was made Governor of the Mount; he bought it in 1659 and his family has been here ever since.

The 14th century Priory Church (the original was destroyed by an earthquake) occupies the highest point of the rocky island. It was thoroughly restored twice in the last century and is now used regularly for public worship. There are two very fine kaleidoscopic rose windows in the east and west walls—glorious jumbles of colour—and also a lovely window of 1914 on the right wall of the chancel which has the Mount in the background, blue and smoky in the distance.

If the thrill of a visit to St Michael's Mount is a little drained by having to move in a crowd, then it floods back a thousandfold when you look down through the trees and suddenly realize that you are on an island. This does not work, of course, if the tide was in when you arrived; but if you walked here over the causeway, then this transformation of the Mount, this first sight of an unbroken stretch of water between you and Marazion, is the best cure in the world for a jaded sense of adventure.

## Porthleven

The harbour at Porthleven is perhaps the most splendid of them all. The complexity and massiveness of the harbour walls give them that Cyclopean look of ancient fortifications. As magnificent as all this stonework may appear, however, Porthleven harbour has always been something of a white elephant.

The name Porthleven means 'smooth harbour', which must surely have been an old Cornish joke for it faces southwest, into the teeth of the prevailing wind, and even in a moderate sea entering the harbour has always been difficult. For centuries Porthleven was just a tiny fishing inlet given a little protection by the rocks and a shingle bar at its entrance, and had it shown any potential for development as a harbour this would certainly have been exploited long ago by the ancient and important town of Helston, two or three miles up the road.

### THE HARBOUR

Porthleven would have remained a poor fishing cove to this day were it not for the late 18th century obsession with harbours of refuge. The increase

27

*'The harbour area is still completely delightful'*

in coastal trade at that time had brought a corresponding increase in wrecks, particularly along the dreaded shore of the Lizard which offered no sanctuary in a southwesterly gale. Porthleven, although far from ideal, was the only possible site for a harbour of refuge along this part of the coast. Public opinion was considerably shaken, and swayed, by the wreck of HMS *Anson* on Loe Bar just a mile east of Porthleven, in the early hours of December 29, 1807. The crowded man-of-war had been trying to weather the fierce storm at anchor, because she could not make it round the Lizard, but eventually drove ashore on Loe Bar when the last of her anchor cables gave way. Crowds lining the clifftops watched, unable to help, as the great ship swung broadside-on to the heavy surf and over a hundred men, women and children were drowned only yards away from the quiet waters of Loe Pool. This tragedy fired local enthusiasm for building a new harbour to which vessels could run in times of distress. In the campaign to promote Porthleven, much use was made of the emotive appeal; the *West Briton* commented in its report in November 1810 of the wrecking of a brig and a Spanish polacre on Loe Bar, that 'we have reason to believe that had the harbour at Porthleven been completed these two vessels would have been saved'.

28

In the following year an Act of Parliament was passed setting up the Porthleven Harbour Company, and the mammoth task began. Formal completion, and the opening of the harbour, was not until 1825 and the works cost £200,000 instead of the estimated £30,000. The problems had included removing the shingle bar at the harbour mouth (380,000 tons of it, which had to be wheeled away in barrows by 70 workmen) and blasting the cliffs to make the entrance wider, as well constructing wharves and one long breakwater in the southwesterly swell.

The infant fishing fleet began to profit from the new harbour almost immediately, and by 1848 there were 63 boats engaged in the mackerel and pilchard fisheries. The Porthleven drifter fleet was one of the top three in Cornwall (along with Newlyn and St Ives), and the ancillary industries which sprang up—fish curing, ropemaking, sailmaking, and particularly boatbuilding and netmaking—were soon renowned far beyond the confines of Cornwall. All the same, the Porthleven fishermen were successful despite their harbour's natural attributes rather than because of them. The situation in January 1853, when the *West Briton* reported that 'it is now thirteen weeks they have not been able to put to sea, owing to the severe gales from the southwest', was probably not all that unusual in the winter months.

The building of Porthleven harbour was not just a humanitarian gesture; it was to have become a port thriving on the trade provided by the local tin, copper and lead mines and the newly discovered china clay deposits at Tregonning Hill. There was the occasional boom, but many of the nearby mines had closed by 1850, and the harbour was never popular with captains and shipowners. Many people believed that it had been, as Davies Gilbert starkly put it, 'a senseless undertaking, which has utterly failed of its object, and made the small harbour less commodious for boats than it was before'.

Porthleven's fortunes changed when the harbour was taken over in 1853 by Messrs Harvey & Co. of Hayle, one of Cornwall's greatest industrial firms. They brought a progressive and positive attitude to their newly acquired lame duck, and created a safe anchorage by building a breakwater and inner basins with wooden baulks, floodgates and sluices on the pattern of their other harbour at Hayle, so that ships could stay afloat at high tides and be protected from southwesterly gales. The sluices were used to scour the harbour, which tended to silt up with mining waste brought down the valley, and were first opened in October 1858.

Boats built by Porthleven shipwrights sailed in the fishing fleets of Scotland and the East Coast, while ketches, sloops and schooners belonging to Porthleven shipowners traded all over the world. In 1866, for example, the *Buenos Aires Standard* carried the following report:

'The descendants of the Pilgrim Fathers cherish with peculiar affection the name of *Mayflower*, the first English vessel that arrived on the shores of New England. In the same manner the inhabitants of the Boca ought to preserve the tradition in future years of the *Ready Rhino*, of Porthleven, which entered the Riachuelo on Thursday, being the first English vessel with cargo that has ever visited that port.'

The 127-ton *Ready Rhino* finally met her end in December 1897 when she foundered off Southwest Wales.

The palmy days did not last long; although the port shipped out china clay until after the First World War, and coal into the 1950s, the 19th century slump in the mines and the insoluble problem of the harbour's orientation saw to it that Porthleven's potential was never realized.

## PORTHLEVEN TODAY

The village is dominated by the magnificent Methodist Church of 1890, which is celebrated with a pithy little verse in Arthur Mee's *Cornwall*:

> They built the church, upon my word,
> As fine as any abbey;
> But then they thought to cheat the Lord
> And built the back part shabby.

Porthleven has also, unfortunately, grown out of all recognition; swollen in undignified fashion into a town to serve the people of Helston and RNAS Culdrose who wanted to live in a fishing village. The harbour area is still completely delightful, however, and hopefully it will always remain so. Sturdy great warehouses crowd about the water's edge, along with the old china clay dry of 1893 (the white arched building on Breageside), the ruined limekiln further down (built in 1805; its owner was foremost in pushing for the new harbour, to protect his investment), and the two waterside pubs—the Harbour Hotel (previously the Commercial) overlooking the inner basin and the Ship Inn, stout but vulnerable near the harbour mouth on Breageside.

Just beyond the Ship Inn you will find the old lifeboat house which dates from 1895 and was in use until the lifeboat station was closed down in 1929. The house is actually in a terrible position: in heavy seas the lifeboat simply could not be launched, and when she could, would often capsize the moment she hit the water. During gales the building used to suffer considerable damage and on one occasion the doors were ripped off and the lifeboat swamped. All the same, it was a distinct improvement on the first lifeboat house which was built in 1863 on the Higher Road, Breageside (now Claremont Terrace), from which the boat had to be drawn on a carriage by four horses down to the harbour. There, provided it was not low tide, when the drop from the jetty was too great, nor so rough that the baulks were down across the harbour entrance, she could then be launched. This old lifeboat on her cumbersome carriage is depicted in a wall painting on the outside of the Harbour Hotel.

On the other side of the harbour mouth from the lifeboat house stands Porthleven's trademark, the Institute and clocktower. Built in 1884 as a Scientific and Literary Institute for the good of all Porthleven citizens, it was given two opening ceremonies and even inspired poetry from Mr Howard Harris, the Schoolmaster:

Kissed by the Summer breeze, and laved by winter's spray
The Institute uplifts its tower with stately grace,
Here rest is found, and science sheds her rays,
A monument of love to bless a future race.

Inevitably, perhaps, it was not long before it was only the males of that 'future race' who were being allowed to enjoy all that rest and science, and the building soon came to be known by all as the Men's Institute.

### UP TO BREAGE

Even if your time in Porthleven is short, Breage Church really must be seen. This sturdy old building with its yellow lichened tower is renowned for its extraordinary 15th century wall paintings which loom vaguely at you from every wall. The limewashed walls and window splays were painted with the series of figures soon after the church's completion in 1466, probably as a form of religious education and carried out by itinerant monastic artists. Somehow these paintings, their colours softly dappled now, have survived being painted over many times since the first purifying days of the Reformation (including one coat of emulsion applied in the 1950s); the work of restoration and cleaning is, with the help of a Murals Appeal, still going on.

## Loe Pool

Most people, when walking from Porthleven, will automatically head in the opposite direction from Breage—and who can blame them, for just a mile away along the cliff path is the glorious surprise of Loe Pool. Here you have an inland lake of fresh, calm, tree-shaded water which is separated from the open sea by no more than a simple (although inexplicable) bank of shingle called Loe Bar. It is such an extraordinary place that inevitably legends abound, such as that which has the undead Jan Tregeagle dropping a sack of sand during one of his impossible tasks, to explain the formation of the Bar; and that which identifies the lake as the 'middle mere' of *Morte d'Arthur* into which Excalibur was cast ('I do not believe a word of it. Arthur was never down there', declared the incomparable Sabine Baring-Gould).

A thousand years ago Loe Pool might have warranted a chapter of its own, because it certainly used to be an estuary open to the sea and navigable as far up as the then port of Helston. It is generally accepted that when the bar finally established itself right across the mouth of the Cober estuary (in the same way as the Doom Bar has always threatened to cross the mouth of the Camel), the citizens of Helston turned their eyes upon Gweek on the Helford River, and began to develop it as their port; the first records of such activity are from the 13th century.

Some 150 years ago, Loe Pool had another chance at fortune when the celebrated engineer J. M. Rendel drew up plans to form a harbour at the mouth of the lake by constructing two huge dams (across the main lake and over Carminowe Creek) along with lock gates, sluices and two great piers, and an industrial complex along the eastern shore. Nothing came of this scheme, and the lake is now completely protected from its modern-day equivalent (Arthurian theme park and out-of-town shopping centre) by the ever-vigilant National Trust.

If you feel like walking to Helston (the west bank is easy going and fairly populous, the east longer and lonelier), the excellent little museum in the old butter market has Rendel's plans on display, along with the plans for Warburton's wonderful wind-powered dredger which he designed to 'fish for tin' in the rich silt at the bottom of Loe Pool. The museum also houses some of the original equipment invented by local man Henry Trengrouse, who had witnessed, with impotent horror, the wreck of the *Anson* in 1807. His rocket life-saving apparatus made an extraordinary difference as for the first time the watchers on the shore had a vital role to play, and it has only recently been improved upon.

*'Fresh, calm, tree-shaded wate*

*Mullion Cove—'The tiny embattled harbour'*

# 2   The Lizard Coves

> I did not know them, but I knew their sea,
> Its pelting flourish by the granite quay . . .

J. C. Trewin, from 'Cornish Boy'

THE harbours of the Lizard are the disregarded coves of the rest of Cornwall. Although this long dark shadow which pushes southwards so far into the English Channel presents a virtual closed door to ships caught in a storm, it was once the home of smugglers to whom every weakness in the cliff face was a potential landing place; and the Lizard's unpromising coves are still the natural harbours for lifeboatmen whose courage is legendary and for fishermen who, as J. R. A. Hockin put it, 'work the Lizard shore as unconcernedly as if it were a river bank'. Behind the coves there is a foreign land of unfamiliar contrasts: tall thatched houses and lush and bloomy gardens; high flat expanses of ancient heathland littered with rare plants and hut circles; quays, stiles, cobbles and churches made from serpentine stone; clear and improbable turquoise water in the shallows surrounding the black rocks of the bay. The most dramatic sight of all in this singular landscape is the Goonhilly Earth Station with its huge silent saucers rising out of the heath, taking their grandeur from the land around them, floodlit at night and shining in the dark unbroken plain, their faces turned up to the moon and a great expanse of stars.

33

## Mullion Cove

At the tiny embattled harbour of Mullion you will find the only artificial protection on this forbidding western flank of the Lizard: two stone piers in a dramatic position with cliffs, rusty black and dusted with green, towering all around, casting great shadows on the turquoise water in the cove below. Offshore lies Mullion Island which, along with the harbour, is now owned by the National Trust. The island forms a natural breakwater, and it was often suggested in the past that the Gap between island and mainland should be blocked to create a good harbour of refuge on this wreck-strewn coast. The island's old name was apparently 'Innis Pruen', which according to the Rev. E. G. Harvey of Mullion, writing in 1875, means 'the Island of round, breast-like protuberances'; sadly, it seems more likely that 'pruen' means something to do with reptiles, vermin or worms rather than breasts.

The small drying harbour at Mullion was not built until 1895; prior to that it was just another rocky cove, with perhaps a little more natural shelter than some, in which a successful pilchard fishery developed against all the odds. A lifeboat station was established here in 1867, long before the breakwaters were built, and the lifeboat seems to have been the only one in Cornwall not provided with a transporting carriage. On returning to the cove after a launch, the boat was winched up the beach on a capstan in a winch house, still there at the head of the beach, and then up the road for a short distance and turned through a right angle before being put back into its house (the second one up from the beach, on the right). When the first lifeboat arrived at Mullion, rocks had to be blasted from the cove entrance and a stream diverted to the north side in order to facilitate launching, both moves being popular with the fishing community too.

Fishing may have been the main occupation here, but it was a fickle way to try to earn a living (between 1859 and 1864, we are told that not a single pilchard was taken at Mullion), and no wonder the people looked to other opportunities offered by the sea. On occasion there were rich pickings to be had from the terrible number of wrecks along the Mullion coast. The splendid Rev. Harvey wrote to the editor of the *Western Morning News* in March 1873 to say that in 'six years and a quarter there have been nine wrecks, with a loss of 69 lives, under Mullyon cliffs'. One of those wrecked ships was the astonishingly named *Jonkheer Meester van der Wall van Putteshoek* which sank off Poldhu Cove in 1867 with a cargo of coffee, arrowroot and tin. Using long tongs and glass-bottomed buckets, the enterprising Mullion fishermen managed to recover the ingots of pure tin from the seabed, and received £15 per ton salvaged for their pains.

Although undeniably dangerous, smuggling was still probably the most dependable employment for the many Lizard fishermen who had strong ties with Brittany, particularly the Roscoff area. The Rev. Harvey left a full account of the freetrade activities of his parishioners' parents and grandparents in his book *Mullyon*: 'and men living may even now, so far from considering it a disgrace, be heard to speak proudly of the day when they were engaged "in the smuggling *service*".' Harvey's *Mullyon* is well worth reading, one of those Victorian books which has increased in richness and charm with its age. In introducing one of his descriptive rambles, for instance, he urges: 'Then come along, let us start from the Vicarage; but first let me put a biscuit or two in my pocket, my little flask of schnaps, and my pocket compass'.

## OVER TO GUNWALLOE

Two miles along the coastal path to the north of Mullion, beyond the coves of Polurrian and Poldhu, you will find one of the most dramatically situated churches in Cornwall. The tiny church of Gunwalloe, its grave-yard within reach of the pounding waves and its detached tower built into the rocky promontory which barely protects this small sanctuary, is constantly threatened with complete destruction by the sea. The *West Briton* of June 30, 1870 gave notice of a bazaar which was to be held in aid of the 'Restoration of this sea-side Church', at a time of particular concern. The revels were to include a military band, the Helston Handbell Ringers, a Public Tea, a Vocal and Instrumental Concert, the Cury Fife Band and 'the Reverend F. C. Jackson's Phantasmagoria Entertainment at eight'. In 1966 a false cliff had to be built north of the church to give it some added protection, and this needs regular repairs and additions of Penryn granite to save it, in turn, from destruction.

Between Gunwalloe Church Cove and Gunwalloe Fishing Cove rises the sombre bulk of Halzephron Cliff. The name, also written Halsferran, comes from the Cornish 'als' and 'yfarn' meaning 'Hell's Cliff', one of the many menacing coast names of the Lizard. At the foot of this bleak cliff many ships have met their end, but it is the wind-cropped brow of Halzephron which has given this place such a macabre reputation: here, in shallow unmarked graves, were buried the victims of shipwrecks over many hundreds of years until the time (1808) when their Christian burial was made a matter of law.

## FROM MULLION TO KYNANCE

The Rev. Harvey wrote of the cliffs between Mullion and Kynance, that 'except the granite uprearing at Tol y Pedn, on the other side of Mount's Bay, you may look in vain for a more splendid bit of cliff between this and the Orkneys'. Many people today would agree with him, and yet even in the height of summer it is quite possible to find yourself alone once you leave behind the attractions of Mullion and step out, high above the sea. The walk along the coast path is about five miles long, and much of this stretch has now been designated a national nature reserve.

The path leads you over Predannack Cliffs where, since 1983, the National Trust and local farmers have, with great sensitivity, been reintroducing cliff grazing during the summer months after a lapse of 25 years, to ensure the return of the rare wild flowers for which these cliffs were once renowned. There are an astonishing nineteen different species of rare and threatened plants here, including six which are only found on the Lizard, for which the grazed cliff habitat is absolutely vital. In a bleak and lonely stretch, the path also crosses the seaward fringe of Predannack Downs, believed to be the oldest area of heathland in the country. Botanists have claimed that every indigenous British heather type can be found here, including the rare Cornish Heath *Erica vagans*. Inland, the Downs are taken up with an airfield where bombers were based during the war but which is now a training aerodrome for RNAS Culdrose.

About two-thirds of the way to Kynance you will come upon Gew-Graze, or Soapy Cove as it is known after the rare deposit of soapstone or steatite which was worked here until about 1850 and went to make fine china. Approaching Soapy Cove from the Kynance side, your first sight is of the perpendicular cliffs to the north falling in great sheets of silver to the kingfisher-blue water far below.

Kynance Cove itself (Kynance means 'ravine') is one of the great draws on the Cornish coast, and as the path drops down and its extraordinary colours and shapes unfold below, it is not hard to see why. Its popularity became established in the Victorian age (appealing to geologists, botanists, climbers and artists as well as mere pleasure-seekers) and excursions were made, often by donkey, from the new hotels of Lizard Town.

## The Lizard and Church Cove

The vulgar development of 'Britain's Most Southerly Point' is a striking example of what would have been the fate of most of Cornwall's coastline were it not for the National Trust. There is no better way to assess the crucial role of the Trust than to visit a place where it has no influence. Tourists who come to the Lizard are adjudged incapable of walking, and so a shimmering car park has been provided for them right on the cliff edge, with two hideous cafés within a few yards. For those in a hurry, there is no need even to unbuckle their seat belts or turn off their engines in order to boast later of a visit to the Point.

Lizard Town, or The Lizard as it is also known, with its offshoots southwards and around Housel Bay, hogs the skyline greedily, but it does have a certain brazen Victorian appeal. It is the unbridled commercial development of *our* century which sounds the truly discordant note. Somehow, the splendour of the Lizard coast still wins through and it is still just possible to take home the memory of sheer cliffs softened by astonishing drapes of wild flowers, of black and awful rocks rearing out of a placid sea, and smaller reefs scattered all around like a rash breaking out on the surface of the water; of the clean white-block buildings of the lighthouse and the old Lloyd's Signal Station, on the far side of Housel; and of the sudden shock of coming upon the Lion's Den, hidden in the coarse grass, a vast hole which an anonymous diarist of 1885 described as being 'about the size, I should say, of Oxford Circus'.

The lighthouse, which is open to the public, has one light which can be seen twenty miles away. Its origins lie in a coal-fired beacon established by

*'The clean white-block buildings of the lighthouse'*

Sir John Killigrew in 1611 and paid for out of his own pocket (it cost about ten shillings a night in coal). The light was unpopular locally because of its success in cutting down on the number of lucrative wrecks.

To the west of the car park and cafés, and the old lifeboat house in Polpeor Cove, and hidden from them all, there is another, older Lizard. At the seaward end of a narrow green lane down from The Lizard, which was 'ye way to Porthpeor' excavated by Mr George Robinson of Cadgwith in 1637 and which is known locally as Rocky Lane, there is an unexpected meadow with a tangled stream, bent tamarisk trees and a rash of mounds dressed thickly in camomile and hogweed. This is Pistol Meadow; the name might come, quite innocently, from the waterfall (Cornish 'pystyll') in the cove below, but it is as doom-laden as the name of Halzephron, for this too is the unhallowed burial ground of drowned sailors. There is a difference, however: the graves here were dug for the dead of one particular wreck, the King's ship *Royal Anne* which was caught up in the turmoil of reefs just offshore in November 1720 and dashed to pieces. Over 200 bodies were later washed ashore around Old Lizard Head and Pistol Cove, and buried in communal pits of twenty or thirty bodies each in the meadow above. There is no doubt that this place has an eerie and deeply melancholy atmosphere but it takes a true son of the Lizard, J. C. Trewin, to describe that feeling:

'And I think, too—at all times—of the meadow and cove so near to us:

37

up the drive, through a rubbed red gate, up Penmenner Lane where the white cats lived, down seaward at the windy corner, along by the house that used to be Maenheere, and right-handed again into the steepest of rocky lanes. This brought you presently to the pasture with the brook, the tang of camomile, the hummocked mounds, and an everlasting sense that you were being watched. If ever a place was haunted, it was Pistol Meadow.'

J. C. Trewin's autobiographical *Up From the Lizard* and *Down to the Lion* are essential, and magical, reading—as much for those people who are as yet unmoved by the Lizard as for those already captivated.

## LANDEWEDNACK

One of the loveliest of Cornish parish names, Landewednack means the church or cell of St Winwaloe (his name in a pet form in this instance), the same dedication as at Gunwalloe. This ancient holy place and its thatched churchtown are tucked into a discreet, sheltered valley above Church Cove. The lovely church has a 13th century castellated porch, a slightly spoilt Norman doorway, and a tower of chequered serpentine and granite blocks. Inside you can buy a copy of an enchanting poem called 'Landewednack Church', penned by the Rector, which begins:

> Dear House of God, whose ancient tower,
> Proud guardian of our English shore,
> Looks westward to the Lizard Downs
> And east across the ocean floor,
> Such work inspired, such craft divine,
> Point to a loftier faith than mine.

## CHURCH COVE

Landewednack's warm hollow where honeysuckle and roses ramble over thatch, and cream teas are on offer in a garden beside the quiet lane, seems very far from the sea; yet, down at the end of the lane is the churchtown's little port. This typically narrow and precipitous Lizard cove used to support a well developed pilchard fishery, a regular trade in coal, depending on the weather and the prevailing wind, a pub called the Mariners in the tall thatched house just above the cove, and for just fourteen years a lifeboat station. The well preserved remnants of such activities are still there, crammed in together above the steep slipway: the large courtyard-type pilchard cellars, the round winch house for hauling the boats up the slip, and the lifeboat house at an angle that made launching so difficult that she only went out on service once during the station's lifetime (1885–99).

A little way south of Church Cove is Kilcobben Cove, another impossible little place dwarfed by green and tumbling cliffs which has been the home of the Lizard–Cadgwith lifeboat since the two stations amalgamated in 1961. Prior to that the Lizard station was at Polpeor Cove (the Church Cove station was a temporary extra) where at first, before the sea-level

*'A surprising number of thatched cottages . . . with the old Huer's House
. . . on the cliff above'*

house was built, the boathouse was on the clifftop: the boat had to be let
down and up on ropes and, in southwesterly gales the crew had to crawl on
their hands and knees to the boathouse to save themselves being blown
over the edge.

## Cadgwith

Cadgwith is one of the few Cornish villages which really is as attractive as
its extravagant reputation claims. It is an enchanting place with a surprising number of thatched cottages, some of them unusually tall, an inn
serving a good selection of seafood, and an uplifting smell of fish lingering
above the cove as a reminder that this is more than just a pretty museum.

The village still bears many traces of a busy past: there is a café in the old
pilchard cellars and a general store in the old watchhouse, and a less
developed collection of lofts and cellars and boathouses, wire, chains,
blocks and winches about the beach, some still in use; the old Huer's
House, from where the pilchard shoals were sighted, is on the cliff above.

In the *West Briton* in 1855 there appeared a glorious description of
Cadgwith when the pilchard fishery was at its height: 'There is a bench
against the white walls of the cottages right in the centre of the village,
from which the whole of the little bay can be seen, and from which the boat

is watched that is perpetually on the look out for signs of pilchards. On this bench the fishermen sit in patience and wait for their harvest—they scarcely turn their eyes from the sea to look at the strangers who pass them. Their interest is all centred on a solitary idea from one year's end to the other, and that idea is the pilchard. It is really very exciting to hear the pilchard cry for the first time; and when visitors are new to the sound, they rise up and leave their dinner or their amusements, and rush out *en masse* to see what is happening. For when a shoal has come within reach, every man who dwells in the village, whatever he may be engaged in doing, is called by a strange and terrible cry to come and help in the "take". And he comes, generally at a gallop, and breathless. The boats are always ready in the bay. The trees in some cases extend down to the water's edge, and are still covered with green foliage. Looking down upon the small scene of excitement from the cliff above, this touch of colour at the marge of the intensely blue Cornish sea adds a wonderful charm. Of course, the real time to see a pilchard take is by moonlight, when the fishes look like living silver, and even the surging mass of life that the fishermen trample down in the boats has a magical effect, that makes one forget the disagreeable side of it.'

That fishermen's bench, known as 'the Stick', is still there, with an unobstructed view of a sadly less productive sea.

## TO CARLEON COVE

A walk northwards along the coastal path from Cadgwith of a mile or so will lead you to Carleon Cove, the early centre of the Lizard's serpentine cutting industry which is now a beautiful, haunted place under the inconspicuous protection of the National Trust. In a rocky green cove at the foot of the unexpected Poltesco valley, where a stream tumbles seawards under bamboo and young trees, just one tall building, restored and dated 1866, remains of the huge complex of factory buildings, chimneys and waterwheels. There is also a lattice of low walls in the scrubland around the Poltesco stream, and strange ruins—wheel pits and sturdy stonework—in every copse and spinney; persistent echoes of a once flourishing industrial centre which employed nearly a hundred people at one time. As Jill Newton has pointed out in her book on the Lizard, you can even see the scoring of saw blades on a flat cutting-stone by the stream.

The round winch house shows that, like all the others, Carleon Cove started off as a fishing cove. The growth of industry here came with the popularity of serpentine with the Victorians. Queen Victoria herself is reputed to have set the ball rolling when she visited the Lizard in the mid-19th century and ordered a serpentine table to be made for her. As the stone became fashionable the factory was set up here, making anything from shop fronts for famous stores in London and Paris to mantlepieces and household ornaments. The works were closed down and the cove reverted to silence after 1893, when individual serpentine workshops, which still operate today, began to be set up in Lizard Town and Landewednack.

## THREE CHURCHES

A little way inland, halfway between Carleon Cove and Cadgwith, is the churchtown of Ruan Minor centred about the school, the parish church and the post office. The little church with its shaggy, creepered tower is plain but surrounded by roses. Inside there is a lovely window, dating from 1926, which has captured exactly that same clear kingfisher blue of the sea in the shallows of the Lizard coves.

Ruan Minor Church escaped the devastation of a full-blooded Victorian restoration, but not so Grade Church, a mile and a half to the west of Cadgwith. This poor building, which can be seen as a landmark for miles around, does retain some charm in its old serpentine tower, and in its isolated position at the end of a crooked green lane still unserved with electricity. In 1861 the main body of the church was in such a bad state of repair that it was demolished and rebuilt disastrously, with the roof being pitched far too high and dwarfing the tower. Charles Henderson, Cornwall's greatest historian, wrote of the rebuilding that 'the cheapness may be excused but the vulgarity never', and W. Boxer Mayne called it an 'architectural nightmare', adding caustically that 'it has little that is noteworthy, unless it be the chancel window remarkable for its ugliness'.

An ugly church may be sad, but at least people still worship there; nothing is more tragic than a ruined church. Ruan Major two miles north of Grade, is now, like the equally melancholy church of Merther above the Tresillian River, almost completely lost; even its fine early 15th century tower seems to have little chance of being saved. The old church, which Henderson considered one of the finest in Cornwall, was, like Grade's, in a terrible state by the 1860s. It too was rebuilt on the cheap, but such an unpopulated area could not support three churches so close together, so the restoration of Ruan Major only postponed for a short time its eventual death.

## Coverack

Unlike almost every other Cornish harbour village, Coverack is not cramped into a meagre hollow in the cliffs but spreads itself in an easy curve, its cottages idling around a wide bay backed by low wooded slopes. Perhaps the loveliest of all Lizard villages, it seems a sunny and generous place, yet the photographs in the bar of the Paris Hotel show how devastating a storm here can be. The harbour itself is tiny and snug, the curl of the hornblende and serpentine wall like a cupped hand sheltering the small fleet of fishing boats beached inside. The good atmosphere at Coverack is enhanced by its car parks which, instead of the ubiquitous 'pay and display' machines, are graced with honesty boxes the money from which goes to local charities.

The friendly Paris Hotel, which sits stoutly right at the end of Dolor Point and has a good little bistro serving local seafood, was named after one of the few wrecks on this coast to have had a happy outcome. In the

*'The curl of the hornblende and serpentine wall like a cupped hand'*

early morning of May 21, 1899, the 10,669 ton American liner *Paris* (bound for New York at great speed with general cargo, a crew of 370 and 386 passengers), ran aground on the rocks at Lowland Point north of Coverack. With daylight, the passengers were able to appreciate their great good fortune when they saw how hideously close were the dreaded Manacle Rocks, the masts and funnel of the reef's latest victim the *Mohegan* still standing out of the glassy water. The passengers were all taken off but the captain and crew remained on board until the *Paris* was finally refloated six weeks later. Extraordinarily, she survived to sail away from a second encounter with the Cornish coast, under her new name of *Philadelphia* in 1914 when she was stranded in thick fog off Rame Head but later refloated almost unscathed.

After the disastrous wreck of the *Mohegan* in 1898 and the stranding of the *Paris* the following year, it was decided by the Lifeboat Institution that another station besides Porthoustock was needed, and Coverack was chosen as the new site. In a letter to the Board of Trade urging just such a course of action, written soon after the *Mohegan* tragedy, the vicar of St Keverne, Canon Diggens made the following point: 'Since lifeboats from distant places cannot work safely and effectually in these (to them) strange and dangerous waters, a second lifeboat should be placed at Coverack. The fishermen at this village are familiar with the Manacles and the boat could be launched in all waters.' The boathouse, with its iron slipway fixed to the projecting rocks of Dolor Point, cost nearly £1800 and took over a year to build; it has now been converted to a restaurant and bakery.

A short walk along a path to the south of Coverack leads past the enchanting row of cottages called Sunny Corner, and on to Chynhalls

Point, capped with the strange lumps and mounds of an Iron Age cliff castle. On the hill high above stands its Victorian descendant, one of those audacious hotels of which, sadly, few are still hotels today, commanding the horizon with an air of shabby dignity.

## THE MANACLES

These rocks, which lie between a quarter of a mile and a mile offshore and extend for a mile northwards from Lowland Point to Porthoustock Point, have a more fearsome reputation than any of Cornwall's other lethal reefs. This reputation is not confined to seagoing circles; the mention of their name, or the sight of them from shore—deceptively small, evil black spines in a calm sea—can make the most stolid of landlubbers shiver. No-one knows how many lives have been lost here, how many ships wrecked, within the sight of safety at Falmouth harbour.

Of all the Manacles' wrecks, the best known and one of the most awful was that of the 7000 ton Hull steamship *Mohegan*. The story of the *Mohegan's* end is full of tragic irony because it seems that her suicidal course, straight for the Manacles, was set early in her voyage down-Channel and was never altered. Although the reasons will never be known because nearly all the officers were drowned, the fact remains that just before seven o'clock in the evening of October 14, 1898, as the passengers were dressed and dining in the elegant saloon, the *Mohegan* was, instead of ten miles off Falmouth, only one mile offshore and heading for destruction at a steady thirteen knots. At the last moment, she changed direction (perhaps the Captain saw the warning rocket put up by the Coverack Coastguard who had seen the massive ship, all lit up, steaming straight for shore) and turned directly into one of the main groups of the Manacles.

The *Mohegan* sank in twenty minutes with the loss of 106 lives, the Porthoustock lifeboat managing to save 44 people in two very difficult trips. Most of the bodies were later washed ashore and many, according to the vicar of St Keverne, were subsequently stripped of their belongings and thus had to be interred without identification. A mass grave in St Keverne churchyard holds most of the dead; it is marked with a stone bearing one word, *Mohegan*. The mystery surrounding the wreck went on to strengthen the old belief that the Manacles have a supernatural magnetism which affects ships' compasses and draws them off course into their rocky clasp.

## Porthoustock

Once no more than a typical fishing cove which indulged in its fair share of smuggling (in June 1792, for instance, Porthoustock men landed an astonishing 218 ankers or over 2000 gallons of brandy in one cargo, without the knowledge of the Revenue men), Porthoustock, pronounced 'Proustock', was transformed by the local road stone trade. The crumbling piers and stone hoppers, like massive gateposts at the entrance to the cove, were built at the end of the last century to ship road stone from the quarries all around. The quarries at Dean Point are still working, and stone is still shipped from the jetties there, but shipments ceased from here in 1958.

The village these days is silent and almost completely unspoilt thanks to the proximity of what used to be a noisy and dusty industry. At the back, towards the wild and bosky valley which runs up to Trenoweth Mill, there is a row of thatched cottages almost swamped by roses and hydrangeas, and by the rickety towers of crab and lobster pots piled outside; at the front, the old lifeboat house (the station was closed in 1942) and a tiny café selling icecream and fresh crab. Cars and brightly painted working boats mingle informally on the grey beach, overshadowed by the massive piers and chasmal quarries which provide such an imposing backdrop to this quiet and unaffected village.

Most of the beach is false, built up from quarry spoil, thus when the lifeboat house was first built the sea was much nearer. As the shore receded over the years wooden rollers had to be used to get the lifeboat launched, and in 1919 a fixed launching way was laid down to the sea.

## Porthallow

'Pralla', as it is known, nestles in a flat-bottomed bowl at the foot of two small valleys just along the coast from Porthoustock, and behind a stony beach littered with coloured open boats. On this beach, within living memory, sailing barges used to land their cargoes of grain and coal on the high tide.

Porthallow was from earliest times the chief fishing village on the Lizard. Some time before 1317, John de Calvo Monte, lord of the manor of Trenoweth, granted to the monks of Beaulieu a plot of land on which to build a cellar for their valuable tithe of fish at 'Porthalou'. The importance of the Porthallow fleet continued as the pilchard fishery became better estabished in the 18th and 19th centuries. In 1832, for instance, a considerable catch was reported: 1400 hogsheads of pilchards were enclosed in one seine net (over four million fish). The overburdened net was then drawn into a convenient place for securing the catch and, fearing that the weight (about 300 tons) might endanger it, another seine was drawn alongside, the full net opened so that some of the fish rushed into the other, and the whole catch was eventually 'tucked' successfully. There is a popular little pub in the village called the Five Pilchards, which serves good seafood sandwiches, and next door the Cellar Marine Garage stands on the site of the old pilchard cellars where the catches were salted and pressed.

# 3  The Helford River

Helford River, Helford River,
Blessed may ye be!
We sailed up Helford River
By Durgan from the sea.

O to hear the hawser chain
Rattle by the ferry there!
Dear, and shall we come again
By Bosahan,
By wood and water fair?


All the wood to ransack,
All the wave explore—
Moon on Calamansack,
Ripple on the shore.

Laid asleep and dreaming
On our cabin beds;
Helford River streaming
By two happy heads;

Helford River, streaming
By Durgan to the sea,
Much have we been dreaming
Since we dreamed of thee.

Dear, and shall we dream
again
The one dream there?
All may go if that remain
By Bosahan,
And the old face wear!

Sir Arthur Quiller-Couch, 'Helford River'

AFTER the rigours of the Lizard coastline, the broad and generous mouth
of the Helford River comes as quite a surprise. With jaws wide open, the
Helford draws in boats by the dozen like a whale drawing in plankton; the
miles of river and creeks have been a harbour of refuge and trade for
hundreds of years and now provide both modern yachting facilities and
peaceful, unspoilt inlets to tempt all those who sail for pleasure.

## Gillan and St Anthony

Just to the south of the Helford River there lurks the old harbour formed by Gillan Creek. Despite its more important neighbour, Gillan harbour occurs in late-medieval port documents and had its own ships trading in fish, hides and slate, and from the 16th century onwards, in tin.

The complete little churchtown of St Anthony-in-Meneage basks on the northern bank, free from a single discordant note, sheltered with boats before and trees behind. That part of the Lizard known as the Meneage also includes the parishes of Manaccan, St Martin, St Mawgan and St Keverne, and the strange Cornish name (pronounced to rhyme with 'vague') identifies it as the Land of Monks. It is quite possible that there was a Celtic monastery or cell here at St Anthony (as there were at many Cornish church sites prior to the Norman Conquest) because a farm by the church bears the ancient name of Lantinning, which means the sanctuary or cell of St Antoninus or 'Entenin'.

The largely 15th century church is famous for its graceful tower, constructed from a type of fine-grained granite not found in Cornwall, so it might well have been brought from Brittany, and for its shining brass candelabra. In 1885 it was in a quite different state from today, as an anonymous visitor to the Lizard commented in his diary:

'. . . on our way today we peeped into St Anthony (a most picturesque little building in a charming spot) and here was a more appalling state of things still. Were it intended to house a litter of pigs it could hardly be considered a tidy sty; and this is a small parish with no poor, an old Vicar (or Rector) who is fairly rich, and yet people can let the house of God fall into this hopeless ruin and squalor! Fie upon them! Fie!'

## MANACCAN

With its unspoilt cottages wandering up a steep slope, Manaccan is one of the most attractive villages in Cornwall. It is also, more significantly, a real village with a permanent population; a friendly, well known pub, the New Inn; a garage, and a church veiled in trees. The church is renowned for the immense fig tree growing out of its walls. In the 1870s it was noted that the tree was 'known to have occupied its present position for at least a century', so it is now very old indeed. Like a similar one in St Newlyn East, the tree is protected by a local legend which warns of dire consequences for anyone who attempts to fell it or even to trim its branches.

## DENNIS HEAD

Gillan Creek is separated from the Helford River by the friendly green paw of Dennis Head. Its position at the mouth of the Helford with its ancient trading posts, and commanding a glorious view over Falmouth Bay, has long been of strategic importance as its old Cornish name (dynas means 'fort') suggests. There was a cliff castle here in the Iron Age; a dyke rampart was thrown across the headland, similar to that on the Dodman and Rame Head further up the coast. Unlike Rame and the Dodman, however, Dennis Head was extensively fortified during the Civil War too, and the remains of ancient ramparts are so mixed up with those of more recent date that it is now impossible to distinguish one era from another.

The Royalist fort on Dennis Head was built by the local lord, Sir Richard Vyvyan, on the orders of Sir Ralph Hopton who, having surveyed all coastal defences in late 1642, considered that a harbour as good as the Helford and so close to the important castle at Pendennis should not be left undefended.

Dennis Fort eventually surrendered to the Parliamentarians, to General Fairfax himself, on March 18, 1646, paving the way for a successful siege of Pendennis which would otherwise have been impossible. A garrison was maintained in the fort for some time after the end of the war because Cornwall remained something of a nursery for Royalist insurgents; in 1647 there were still 100 men stationed here. All that remains today of this important military stronghold is a confusion of mounds and trenches beneath a sweet-smelling blanket of gorse.

## The Helford River

Beyond the little private coves with their colour-washed wooden boat-houses and beyond the haze of masts between Helford and Helford Passage, you can see the curves and folds of the river opening up ahead. This beautiful estuary would have been a very different place today had it not been situated so close to the outstanding natural harbour of Falmouth. Instead of becoming a famous harbour in its own right, the Helford was renowned as a haven for pirates. In this century, the echoes of a romantic buccaneering past which linger on in the twisting creeks and impenetrable woods have inspired many writers, notably Daphne du Maurier (*Frenchman's Creek*) and Q (*Sir John Constantine*).

These days, Cornish pirates would be unable to afford to live around the Helford River, unless they were particularly successful ones. This is a playground for the rich: the boats bobbing at anchor and the houses which peep out from the trees are noticeably larger and grander than is usual in Cornwall. Development is not rampant, however, and much of the river is almost uniquely unspoilt. The preservation of the Helford's natural beauty is no accident; the very fact that it is such a remarkable place suggests that unusual forces have been at work. The contribution that one good landowner can make, and the legacy he can leave behind after he has gone, has been described by C. C. Vyvyan in the unforgettable portrayal of 'The Old Landlord' in her much loved book *The Helford River*:

'His method of dealing with problems is sometimes described as "taking the long view" and assuredly, in his dealings with the Helford and its unspoilt beauty, he took the long view, not from force of habit but from a deep conviction about what was due from himself to the river . . . It was not for him, a mere single-life guardian of the river, to allow any little creature of a day to squat upon those shores in a pert bungalow; it was not

47

for him to permit the erection of any building that would break in on the quietness of those fields and slopes of bracken, on the reflections of those clouds and trees, on the solitude of those herons, ducks, gulls and curlews.'

The Old Landlord, who is never entirely identified in the book, was the author's husband Sir Courtenay Vyvyan of Trelowarren, who died in 1941.

## TO DURGAN AND MAWNAN

A short way along the coastal path from Helford Passage to Durgan you will pass the private Trebah Beach in Polgwidden Cove. It was one of the many beaches in the Falmouth area which were used by the Americans in the last war for embarkation on D-Day. Behind the beach, sub-tropical gardens rise up and away from the river to the small 18th century house of Trebah (pronounced *Tree*-ba) at the head of the valley. The breathtaking gardens—a riot of colour and rare species—are open to the public on Sundays throughout the summer.

The tiny fishing hamlet of Durgan, its waterfront dominated by its old school and chapel, is now partly owned by the National Trust. Like so many estuarine and coastal villages without harbours, Durgan still indulged in its fair share of coastal trade; the old sailing barges and schooners simply used to beach on the foreshore to load and unload cargo between tides. Durgan's wonderful backdrop of trees is part of the wooded valley garden of Glendurgan, also owned by the National Trust and open to the public on Mondays, Wednesdays and Fridays from March to October.

Further on along the coastal path, the tower of Mawnan Church can just be seen poking through the trees above the shaley cliffs beyond Toll Point, the smooth hump that is the Helford's other gatepost. This bald-block church, snuggled in woodland, lies a mile south of the rapidly expanding village of Mawnan Smith on the possible site of an Iron Age fort which, together with Dennis Head, would have provided a pretty formidable defence of the mouth of the Helford.

## Helford

This idyllic village, huddled in an inlet on the southern shore of the main river, was once so busy a port that it supported a Custom House of its own, as did Gweek at the head of the river. In 1724 Daniel Defoe visited Helford during his tour of the whole of Britain, and wrote: 'At Helford is a small but good harbour . . . where many times the tin-ships go in to load for London; also here are a good number of fishing vessels for the pilchard trade, and abundance of skilful fishermen'.

A description of the port written ninety years later mentions the extensive and substantial stone quay where vessels of over 300 tons might load and unload, and on which stood a cellar suitable for any kind of merchandise. This would have included corn, timber, limestone and coals, but Helford's potential for expansion in trade was limited by the difficulty of land carriage in the hilly country behind it.

*Durgan—'Its waterfront dominated by its old school and chapel'*

Helford's inevitable popularity with visitors has been handled unusually well by those in charge of its development. The car park, for instance, is hidden from the river by trees—a welcome change from those glaring metallic rows which so often spoil a beautiful scene. Mind you, this is no longer a Cornish village; there is that tell-tale neatness about the place (even the lobster-pots look ominously clean) and two-thirds of the 68 houses are empty in winter. As at Cadgwith this is just a more extreme example of the trend throughout Cornwall, as the Cornish are driven inland by the criminally high prices which others will pay for a picturesque coastal property.

One of the great draws at Helford is the famous, but completely unassuming, Riverside Restaurant which has an international reputation for its seafood in particular, and a friendly informal atmosphere. Cream teas are served at Rose Cottage, on the far side of the stream, where the tea itself is as good as the setting and the view—a combination rarely achieved.

Just beyond Helford Point is the Helford River Boatyard which, although not out of danger, was recently saved from demolition and redevelopment by the joint opposition of the National Trust, the Council for the Protection of Rural England and the Helford River Association, taking on together the role of the Old Landlord.

## Porth Navas

Between the famed cockle bed on the Bar, by Helford Passage, and the great eiderdown of Calamansack Wood, Porthnavas Creek ambles away to the north. This creek was called 'Cheilow, alias Calamansake' by Leland in the 16th century, and was still written Chielow on Martyn's map of 1748, but it now takes the name of the village which is tucked into an inlet halfway along its length, the name meaning the cove or harbour of the sheep.

These days, Porth Navas (or Port Navas) is famous not for sheep but for oysters, the Duchy Oyster Farm being just by the old granite quay at the entrance to the inlet. It is now run by Len Hodges, a fourth generation oysterman who is attempting to put the fishery back on its feet after a recent lean time, and is even diversifying into mussels and clams. Here oysters from the Fal are relaid on the river bed for a long process of purifying and fattening before being sold on; the oyster beds are the much-welcomed open stretches of water marked by thin sticks. Helford oysters are renowned the world over for their plumpness and sweetness, and the oyster fishery is an ancient industry which still employs local people and demands from them the same old skills and practices. Tragically, a disease endemic to the Pacific oyster has spread to this area in recent years. This disease kills oysters and there is no cure; those unaffected remain perfectly safe to eat, but they have been few and far between. There have recently been signs that the disease may be dying out here, although it is early days yet for optimism, but Mr Hodges has faith in the future of his oyster farm and in the clear waters of the Helford.

Porthnavas Creek is the last area of new building on the Helford. Upriver, beyond all development and most habitation, the wooded folds recede into the distance, beckoning you on towards that lightening in the sky that marks the west. Back to the east there is the breathtaking view of the river mouth. 'There is something inexpressibly beautiful about that view', C. C. Vyvyan wrote. 'It seems as if that long horizon where sky and water meet were calling you to sail away to southern seas, to wander on and on until you could overlook the far rim of the universe.'

## Frenchman's Creek

Just a little upriver from Helford, the most famous creek of all pierces the Helford's southern shore. At first, it seems remarkable only for its un-Cornish straightness and its completely unspoilt wooded banks, and yet there is an atmosphere here which is remote and enigmatic. It is not easy to decide whether this is due to Daphne du Maurier's novel, or whether the feeling was always here and actually inspired her to write her memorable tale.

Even though the creek's east bank is open to the public, thanks to the National Trust, and thus you might meet several other people walking beside the green water on a summer's day, this place retains the intense and private air so hauntingly described in *Frenchman's Creek:*

'The solitary yachtsman who leaves his yacht in the open roadstead of Helford, and goes exploring upriver in his dinghy on a night in midsummer, when the nightjars call, hesitates when he comes upon the mouth of the creek, for there is something of mystery about it even now, something of enchantment. Being a stranger, the yachtsman looks back over his shoulder to the safe yacht in the roadstead, and to the broad waters of the river, and he pauses, resting on his paddles, aware suddenly of the deep silence of the creek, of its narrow twisting channel, and he feels—for no reason known to him—that he is an interloper, a trespasser in time. He ventures a little way along the left bank of the creek, the sound of the blades upon the water seeming over-loud and echoing oddly among the trees on the far bank, and as he creeps forward the creek narrows, the trees crowd yet more thickly to the water's edge, and he feels a spell upon him, fascinating, strange, a thing of queer excitement not fully understood.'

You can walk to Frenchman's Creek, or Pill as it is known locally, from Helford village along a number of footpaths, all of which lead to Kestle (once the principal manor of the parish). From here a rocky old green lane drops down to the head of the creek through the thick woods, wild green and full of birdsong and the smell of wild garlic.

## Polwheveral Creek

Just beyond Frenchman's Creek the Helford River is split by Groyne Point, and Polwheveral Creek curls off to the north while the main river keeps on its westward way towards Gweek. Polwheveral Creek (the name means 'lively stream') is particularly remote and rural; much of its unspoilt shoreline and that of its offshoot Polpenwith Creek is protected, although not owned, by the National Trust.

On the point of land between the two creeks there is an old wharf called Scott's Quay which in the last century turned this silent stretch of water into a great artery of trade. Scott's Quay was the main shipping point for the Constantine stone trade which flourished well into this century: in 1935, for instance, there were no less than eight granite quarrying firms operating in the parish. The old packhorse track by which the stone was carried straight down to the quay still has the status of a public right of way and can be followed right up to Constantine, a walk of just over a mile through a really lovely piece of rural Cornwall.

## Merthen

Merthen Wood, which covers the northern bank of the Helford upriver from Groyne Point, is perhaps the most perfect stretch of woodland in the whole of Cornwall. In the thick all-enveloping roll of the summer months, there is not a branch to be seen, no wisp of brown poking through or chink of light from the underwood, just a flawless quilt of mellow oak green.

The wood is probably a shrunken remnant of an oak forest which once covered all the southern part of Constantine parish, and is certainly part of the great spread of woodland (1 league long and 1½ leagues wide) recorded in Domesday Book in 1086 under the King's manor of Winnianton, which at that time included Merthen. It consists almost entirely of small coppice oak, cut regularly since the 16th century when the growth of mining necessitated large quantities of charcoal for the smelting of tin in the blowing-houses (the nearest to Merthen being at Gweek and at Polwheveral). Deep in the woods the charcoal burners worked, the finished product being lighter to transport than the cut wood, and in many old coppice woods you can still find the charcoal pits, circular areas about 15 feet in diameter with smooth level floors of earth or ashes, where the skilfully built stacks of wood used to burn, very slowly, for between two and ten days.

The name Merthen means in Cornish 'sea fort'; on the hill above the woods, with a dramatic view down the Helford to the sea, are the two rectangular enclosures of an ancient fort which perhaps once helped to guard the upper reaches of the river. The manor house of Merthen, hidden behind the woods, has long been the principal place on the river, and the lords of Merthen have claimed jurisdiction over the higher creeks from a very early date. In the ditch on the western side of the fort runs the ancient ridgeway road from Merthen Quay northwards over the Downs, in some places taking the form of a sunken green lane, and in others no more than a shallow indentation in the side of a field.

Merthen Quay, tumbling and grass-grown with massive granite blocks strewn nonchalantly about, used to have a good trade in woodland products like charcoal, and in oysters, and in limestone which was landed here and burned in the limekilns alongside (now overgrown and ruined). It also was the highest point reached by the big Norwegian timber ships which brought the mining timber in the 18th and 19th centuries. The ships used to anchor here in the deep water of Merthen Hole where their cargoes were unloaded into barges from Gweek and transported up to the timber pools near the head of the river.

## Tremayne

All of the Merthen land is private, but the pale sunlit Tremayne Woods on the opposite bank are owned by the National Trust and there is a lovely walk between the Mawgan–Manaccan road (a fine walk in its own right) from a point near Mudgeon, and Tremayne Quay just downriver from Merthen Quay.

Tremayne Quay was built by Sir Richard Vyvyan especially to receive the disembarking Queen Victoria on her proposed visit to Trelowarren in 1846, which then never took place. However, there must have been some sort of earlier quay, either here or upriver, because in 1814 a bill of sale for the mansion of Tremayne noted that its situation was 'admirably well calculated for establishing a Pilchard Fishery; the Cellar would serve for holding the Salt and curing the Fish, and the Quay for shipping them off'.

Half a mile upriver from Tremayne Quay, the woods skirt the eastern bank of Vellan Tremayne Creek (meaning the creek of Tremayne Mill). Between the head of this creek and the road, the path climbs gently through a valley of astonishing lushness: the steep sides and narrow floor wild and luxuriant in dappled sunlight with old trees towering above—chestnut, oak, beech, lime and holm oak all reaching extraordinary heights, while the sea is so near that the strong salt smell hangs in their branches and drifts about their roots.

## UP TO GEAR

This path through the Vellan Tremayne valley is part of an ancient route from the hill fort at Caer Vallack down to a landing-place at the head of the creek. Just to the north of the small Caer Vallack, on the hill high above Bishop's Quay (an old commercial wharf on the Helford), there is the largest and most perfect earthwork in Cornwall, called Gear (meaning 'fort').

There are many earthworks around the shores of the Helford, indicative of its importance in ancient times, but nothing quite like this one which encloses an area of fourteen acres. Its size and fine defensive position led to its unexpected occupation, centuries after its abandonment, by a group of Cornish rebels in 1648. The 'Gear Rout', as the insurrection came to be known, was a Royalist rebellion, two years after the end of the Civil War, which began in the Penzance–Gulval–Helston area in mid-May and lasted for about ten days before the rebels were scattered by troops from Helston and Penzance.

## TRELOWARREN

The Vyvyans have lived at Trelowarren, one of the loveliest of Cornwall's great houses, for an astonishing 550 years, and now share it with an ecumenical charity called the Trelowarren Fellowship. The house has become a centre for many branches of the arts and has also, with a rare sense of taste and dignity, been developed to appeal to the wider general public, with a pottery, a gift and book shop, a gallery which hosts regular exhibitions by the Cornwall Crafts Association, a camping site and a herb nursery among its attractions. There is also a very fine little restaurant, the Yard Bistro, in the old carriage house.

The whole estate is a real joy to visit; it is a place of great peace and a timeless unity of which C. C. Vyvyan wrote so evocatively in *The Old Place*:

'I sometimes wonder if that long-drawn out association of men with this particular spot of land may partly explain a curious sense . . . of unity between the house and its immediate surroundings'.

# Gweek

Beyond Mawgan Creek the channel swings from side to side between Bonallack Wood on the one hand and unblemished farmland on the other.

*'Gweek still turns its face to the river . . .'*

Silting from the mining districts to the north and west has lessened the river's navigability; as the quays which here begin to crowd the banks suggest, Gweek was once a busy port. Hidden deep within the country, with nearly six miles of hill-bound river protecting it from the open sea and threats of raids and piracy, Gweek was in the perfect position for a port in ancient times, as was Lostwithiel on the Fowey and Tregony on the Fal.

Gweek began by serving the old tin-mining district of 'Kirrier' and at least three routeways lead to the port from the tin area. By the 14th century it was taking on a new role as the harbour for Helston, once that old port had been cut off from the sea by Loe Bar. Its golden age came two centuries later when there was a great expansion in tin mining in this area and Gweek not only exported most of the tin but smelted much of it too. A general coastal trade was carried on steadily through the centuries, unaffected by those vagaries in Cornwall's mining fortunes which could mean that a shipload of tin one year might become a shipload of emigrating miners the next. There is a memorable description of Gweek in 1890 in Lane's *Guide to the Helford:*

'There are generally a few coasters lying high and dry, discharging coals, bricks, tiles and other like merchantise, with masts and yards embroidered in the overhanging foliage, and at low tide, the impression is unavoidably given that the craft have been stranded for years, and it seems strange they could manage to penetrate so far inland, and the idea is not dispelled until you see one or two of a living crew on the end of the topsail yard, picking some fruit from the neighbouring branch of an apple tree.'

Unlike most other land-bound old ports, Gweek still turns its face to the river, and enough boats and boatyards remain to help the little place retain its charm, despite some tactless new building.

# 4  The Fal Waterway

We are in a very wild and barbarous place which no
human being ever visits, in the midst of a most
barbarous race, so different in language and custom
from the Londoners and the rest of England that
they are as unintelligible to these last as to the
Venetians.

The Venetian Ambassador to Castile, writing from Falmouth
where he had been delayed by storms, in 1506.

FALMOUTH Harbour is one of the finest natural havens in the world, and
the third largest after Sydney and Rio. The estuary with all its many creeks
has a total shoreline of nearly 70 miles; there is a place to suit everyone
somewhere along that waterfront—from the most silent, secret inlets
where herons stand and swans glide and man is an intruder, to the
vibrance and energy of a working port and holiday resort with a crowded
marina and bustling main street. This is a paradise for anyone afloat for
there is enough exploration and discovery to excite the most experienced
sailors, yet a trip from Falmouth or Malpas in a sturdy river cruiser is safe
enough to tempt all steadfast inland souls onto the water.

From earliest times, the estuary has been a harbour of refuge for all
Channel shipping, and every creek and quay had its own coasting trade.
The Black Rock at the harbour entrance has long been a danger to

shipping and has been marked by a beacon since the 16th century. It was also, according to that master storyteller Sabine Baring-Gould, the scene of a dastardly piece of marital malpractice at some time in the past:

'An eccentric Mr Trefusis, of Trefusis opposite Falmouth, one day invited his wife to boat with him to the Black Rock and picnic there. She incautiously accepted, and when he had landed her, he made his bow and rowed away with "Madam, we are mutually tired of each other, and you will agree with me that it were best to part". Fortunately a fishing-smack picked her off just as the tide was flowing over it, and brought her back to Trefusis. "Be hanged to you rogues," said the husband. "I'd have given you a guinea each to let her drown; now you shan't have a shilling from me."'

It would be satisfying to be able to report that the damp but spirited Mrs Trefusis then gave the fishermen a guinea to dump her husband on the rock, which was by now covered by a boisterous sea, but the story sadly ends there; the rest is wishful thinking.

## Falmouth

In Leland's day, there was nothing on the site of the town of Falmouth but the Killigrew house Arwenack and a few fishermen's cottages, a hamlet called Smithick or Pennycomequick. The remains of the house on Arwenack Street, much of which was burned down in the Civil War, have been saved and repaired since 1978 by Percy Williams & Sons of Redruth. The fishing hamlet was probably centred on what is now Market Strand and The Moor, which was then a tidal inlet up as far as the Berkeley Vale of today. Penryn and Truro were the main ports on the estuary, and the castles of Pendennis and St Mawes, which were in the process of being built, were there largely to protect Penryn from Spanish and French attacks.

Falmouth was a planned town, the Killigrew family's baby. A twinkle in successive Killigrew eyes from the beginning of the 17th century onwards, the infant port was finally baptised by Royal Proclamation in 1660: Smithick alias Pennycomequick became Falmouth. In the following year the charter of incorporation was granted. The huge potential of a harbour town sited by deep water at the estuary mouth, now that the threat of seaborne attack was lessened by the presence of the two castles, was as obvious to Penryn and Truro as to the Killigrews, but the frantic oppositon of the two towns could do nothing to halt Falmouth's precocious development. In 1670 the Customs House Quay, now a listed structure, was built by Sir Peter Killigrew, and improvements came thick and fast until in 1688 the port had reached the point when it could be considered, and eventually chosen, as a prestigious packet station by the Postmaster General, in preference to Plymouth or Fowey. Falmouth's palmy days had begun.

## THE PACKET STATION

At first, the Post Office's packet ships carried their cargo of mails, passengers, goods and despatches to and from Spain and Portugal only, but the service was later expanded to include North and South America and the West Indies, although routes and destinations varied constantly with the fluctuations in foreign policy.

The forty or so packet ships (sleek, swift brigantines with a crew of about 30), which undertook an average of 100 voyages a year, were popular targets for pirates because they carried money for business transactions as well as ordinary letters. Falmouth's excellent little maritime museum, housed next door to the old packet office, displays a good collection of information on the packet service and on some of its more colourful characters, famous ships and exciting escapades. The atmosphere of Falmouth at that time was captured by Lord Byron, among others, who was here in 1809 awaiting the packet bound for Lisbon, and who wrote a high-spirited poem to his friend Hodgson from 'Falmouth Roads'.

The decline of the Packet Service here at Falmouth began after the Napoleonic Wars, when control was transferred from the Post Office to the Navy and most of the general packet ship repair work started to go to Devonport. The decline continued with the gradual replacement of sail with steamers, and the removal of one route after another to other ports, particularly Southampton. In January 1851 the last service was taken over, and Falmouth ceased to be a packet port.

## FALMOUTH TODAY

To look at it today you would hardly think that the town had suffered such a dramatic setback to its development only last century. In 1851, Falmouth must have been a very depressed and insecure place. Fourteen years later, Alphonse Esquiros witnessed the coming of the railway to the town. It was an event greeted with great celebrations and decorations but still tainted by the loss of the packet service.

'It is certain, that the recently-opened railway will make a new town of Falmouth, and all it wants now is to get back the service of the transatlantic mail boats.'

They never came back, but Falmouth was still unusually rich in natural assets, and the development of its general trade, its shipbuilding and repair industries and the important pilchard fishery had been progressing steadily all the time. It was in ship repair in particular, as an inevitable development of Falmouth's age-old role as a refuge for storm casualties, and in the expansion of the docks that the town's future was to lie.

Despite all Falmouth's problems, there is undeniably a vitality here— the incomparable vitality of a working port. The town itself goes 'flouncing about the hillsides with gaudy uncorseted growths from Penryn to Maen Porth' (J. R. A. Hockin, sharp and elegant as ever) and, as with most harbour towns, the fairest face of Falmouth is reserved for those approaching in a boat. This lively and colourful view has, amazingly, been enhanced rather than ruined by new developments: the clever 'licorice allsort' jumble of new houses and flats actually adds to the delights of the waterfront scene.

## UP TO PENDENNIS

There can be few better places in the world from which to catch the excitement and splendour of working dockland than Castle Drive, which forms a gallery above the huge dry docks, cranes and wharves, the massive tankers and liners, and the old warehouses, fitting shops and foundries of Falmouth Docks, against the unrivalled backdrop of Trefusis Point and Carrick Roads. It is the grandest view I know. To the left of the docks is Bar Pool; once the centre of Falmouth's boatbuilding industry, it used to support smithies, timber yards and seasoning ponds, launching slips and a tide mill which had become a ruin in 1900. Beyond Bar Pool, Falmouth spreads out and up alongside the Penryn River, or the King's Road as it used to be called, with Flushing on the far bank.

Out on the tip of Pendennis Point, a little beyond Crab Quay, there is a Tudor blockhouse called Dennis Fort or Little Dennis. It was built before Pendennis and dismantled in 1654, but quite a substantial shell remains and if you prefer to visit Tudor fortifications on your own you would do better to stay here rather than make your way uphill to Little Dennis's celebrated successor.

Both Pendennis, built on the site of an Iron Age fort, and St Mawes Castles formed part of a string of coastal forts built by Henry VIII as a response to the reconciliation, in 1538, between Spain and France, our traditional enemies whose continued rivalry English diplomacy had, until then, been successfully fostering. Ironically, the most important episode in the castle's life was the ability of the 900 strong garrison to hold out for five months against fellow countrymen during the Civil War. The governor of the castle at the time was the 70-year-old Colonel Arundell, and the Parliamentary forces could do nothing to make him surrender until August 17, 1646 when food had all but run out, and even then he managed to negotiate the full honours of war for his men and an almost triumphant exit from the castle.

Beyond Pendennis, the road curls around the shore of Falmouth Bay towards the beaches of Gyllyngvase and Swanpool. This is the hotel quarter, and king of them all is the Falmouth Hotel, a massive sculptured cream cake of a place around which all the others cluster in dowdy imitation.

## Penryn

Penryn is a hectic town (although there is always peace to be found down a side street), but nothing should deter you from just standing still for a moment to see the loveliness of the granite buildings. If the town seems attractive and well cared for to an unusual degree, it is because it was designated a Housing Action Area in 1975 due to its appalling slum conditions, and over 200 houses built between 1650 and 1800 have been restored since then. The chief architect of Carrick District Council has claimed that Penryn is the first town in the world to be fully restored, as opposed to being rebuilt; to a lay person it seems to have been a dramatically successful project. St Thomas Street, for instance, which is part of the old road from Falmouth, must now be one of the loveliest streets in Cornwall.

## PENRYN AS A PORT

The name Penryn means 'promontory' or 'point of land', and this perfectly describes its position climbing a narrow hill between the two arms of the creek. The town was originally a speculation by the bishops of Exeter—they built it in one of their parks—but it owed its growth and prosperity to maritime trade. Until the development of Falmouth, Penryn and Truro were the main ports on the Fal, and Penryn soon had the cosmopolitan atmosphere of a busy trading harbour; in 1327 half of the people living in the town were foreigners. The port's overseas contacts were not always peaceful, however; inevitably, it was subject to attacks from Spanish and French pirates from time to time. Leland described Penryn's defences against such attacks as 'Stakes and Foundations of Stone sette in the Creeke at Penrine afore the Toun, a little lower than wher it brekith into Armes . . . a Gap in the Midle of the Stakes, and a Chain'.

Piratical activities were not, of course, confined to aliens, and some of the most active local pirates were members of the eminent Killigrew family—Falmouth's patrons. Particularly interesting are the stories of two Killigrew wives: one, Mary Knyvet, led a midnight raid on a Spanish ship in 1583; the other, Lady Jane Killigrew, boarded two Hanseatic ships in Falmouth harbour with a gang of men and plundered them. Lady Jane's story has surely suffered from centuries of distortion by male historians—a modern one, for instance, dubs her 'amateur pirate and faithless wife' (whereas the male Killigrew pirates were, of course, dashing and professional)—but it is known that at some time after her loyal and heroic husband had divorced her, she sought the protection of the Borough of Penryn. In recognition of the sanctuary she found here, Lady Jane presented the mayor with a silver loving-cup, which is still treasured today, inscribed with the words: 'From Maior to Maior. To the Town of Permarin when they received me that was in great misery. J. K. 1633.' She is said to have lived during her stay in what is now called Queen Anne Cottage in St Thomas Street, a listed building dating back to about 1500.

## GLASNEY

In those early days, Penryn's main quay area was on the southern arm of

59

the creek which ran up towards Glasney College. This establishment was founded by Bishop Bronescombe of Exeter in 1265; the actual site was revealed to him in a vision by St Thomas à Becket, who must have had little knowledge of building because the place he indicated was most unsuitable, with a marshy subsoil necessitating constant repairs and reconstruction. The college became a centre of ecclesiastical learning famous all over Europe, despite the fact that the canons seemed to spend a good deal of time poaching in the bishop's deer park. The college buildings must have been magnificent—they had three strong towers of granite and Caen stone—and the grounds were walled and fortified.

Glasney was gradually demolished from 1549 onwards, after its dissolution, and the last few buildings were pulled down in the 18th century. Stone from Glasney is now distributed, in equitable fashion, all over the town, and discovering the odd bit of dressed stone or a gargoyle or pillar or archway tucked away in Penryn's gardens and alleys is almost more exciting than having the whole college laid out before you in pristine condition.

## THE FOOTPATH TO FLUSHING

If the chaos of the town becomes too much, there is no better retreat than the footpath which runs along the northern bank of the main creek, below Penryn's parish church of St Gluvias. Here the traffic sounds recede; close to, only the hollow bangings of people working on their boats echo across the water. This is the place from which to appreciate how Penryn is laid out, climbing the ridge up and away from its quays and wharfs. Here you can sit in peace and contemplate the fine collection of warehouses on the water's edge opposite, along Commercial Road. That was the chief business area of the 18th and 19th centuries with quays, storehouses, chandleries, merchants' offices, coalyards and limekilns. Penryn had to become a highly diversified industrial centre after the development of Falmouth as a far superior port.

Penryn's most important industry and main export, however, was granite from the quarries around the town. The river frontage from the new bridge across the southern creek (there used to be a swing bridge here) down to where 'Harveys' is now was once taken up with the stonemasons' yards belonging to the Freemans (later, Freeman and McCleod) who controlled much of the Cornish granite industry. Granite dressed here was shipped all over the world and was used to build much of Penryn as well as London Bridge, the Suez Canal, the Fastnet Lighthouse, the docks at Buenos Aires, Calcutta, Singapore, Simons Bay, Gibraltar, Colombo and Famagusta, and in this century London's South Bank complex.

The walk from Penryn to Flushing is a must for all boat enthusiasts; along this first stretch of river, and in the remoteness of Sailor's Creek further on, you will pass a wonderfully eccentric collection of craft in various stages of repair, with the furry wrack-clad ribs of those beyond help breaking surface in between. Wherever you find a number of old boats gathered together, it is always from the most decomposed and unseaworthy hulks that you will hear emerging the constant crackle of the shipping forecast, such is the essential optimism of the devotees of old wooden boats.

Just before joining the road at Flushing, the path passes the historic boatyard at Little Falmouth, now occupied by Falmouth Boat Construction Ltd. In the 17th century there was a pilchard cellar here, called Lobb's Palace, and the site was developed as a shipbuilding centre from 1758 onwards by the Symons family, who also had yards at Bar Pool in Falmouth, and later by the great shipwright H. S. Trethowan.

## Flushing

Just across the river from Falmouth, yet miles away in spirit, is the warm and peaceful village of Flushing. This popular, yet relatively unspoilt, place has the quiet elegance of a miniature spa town; the buildings are not grand, but nearly all are pretty with lots of hung slate and an attention to detail unusual in Cornish fishing villages. St John's Street, in particular, has some very fetching houses.

The plan and look of the village has changed very little over the years; this is often the case with a settlement planned and controlled by a powerful local patron. In this instance the fairy godfather was Francis Trefusis. He transformed the hamlet of Nankersey into the little town of Flushing in the 17th century, with the help of Dutch engineers from Flessinghe (hence the name) who supervised the draining of low-lying marshland and the building of sea walls and quays. New Quay, at the end of St John's Street, was built later to protect the village from southeasterly gales.

Although the Trefusis family had hoped to create a rival to Falmouth, Flushing's inhabitants were almost entirely dependent on the port across the water. The men who lived in Flushing were mostly seamen on packet ships, merchant ships and naval ships; the rest were fishermen, ferrymen and bargemen. The families of packet captains and naval officers, in particular, were encouraged by the Trefusis family to settle in Flushing and they lent to the village an un-Cornish air of gentility and sophistication which it has never completely lost. James Silk Buckingham, who was born here in 1786, gives this memorable description of Flushing in his autobiography:

'. . . in its greatest days, between 1790 and 1795, there was probably no place in England which for its size produced so much gaiety and elegance of life as did this little village. Dinners, balls and evening parties were held at some one or other of the Captain's houses every evening, and not a single night passed in which there were not three or four dances at the more humble places of resort for the sailors and their lasses. Scarce a Sunday passed without the gay scene of a wedding at Mylor church.'

The loss of the packet service must have dealt a devastating blow to Flushing: the population shrank from 1250 in 1841 to 850 just ten years later, but the village was saved from complete ruin by an opportune expansion of the pilchard and oyster fisheries.

## OUT TO TREFUSIS POINT

The road from New Quay to Kiln Quay, the old private landing place of the Trefusis family, is also the access road for Flushing's Victorian ghetto where there are to be found some very individual houses. With its lush, south-facing gardens, the private slipways, high walls and hedges, the turrets, battlements and parapets, this is a film producer's paradise. The most astonishing of all, perhaps, is the one at the far end, a mock-Tudor fantasy looking good enough to eat, wrapped in the soft sylvan darkness of Kiln Wood.

It is only a short walk from the end of Trefusis Road to Trefusis Point, and the full view of Carrick Roads. This grand stretch of water always looks rather surprising and out of place; a long regular slab of sea cut into a narrow and crooked land. There is also a dramatic contrast between the two rims of this giant's bathtub: this eastern side is generally rather built up, especially to the north, whereas the far side, apart from some ugly skyline development above St Just, is bald fields and tawny scrubland, retaining that remoteness so characteristic of the Roseland peninsula as a whole.

Beyond Trefusis Point, the path carries on towards Mylor and passes a granite pillar marking the boundary between the harbours of Truro and Falmouth. On the far side of the Carrick Roads a similar pillar stands on Messack Point near St Just. Truro's limits originally extended to the Black Rock at the sea entrance, but Charles II punished the town for sympathising with the Parliamentary cause during the Civil War by giving the new port of Falmouth jurisdiction right up to the junction of the Fal and Truro Rivers. The present compromise was established in the reign of Queen Anne.

## Mylor

The harbour here is so dominated by boats that it is considered dangerous to enter the village unless you are wearing yachting gear. It owes its substantial quays to the Admiralty; a dockyard was established here at the beginning of the 19th century, taking advantage of the deep sheltered water of the creek, which Norden, writing in the late 16th century, identified as 'Melor Poole, wherein the greatest shippe that sayles may ryde saufe'.

The dockyard was used for supplying stores, water and fresh vegetables to the ships of the Royal Navy throughout the Napoleonic Wars, and again during the Crimean War in the 1850s when it also carried out some ship repair work. The training ship HMS *Ganges* was supplied from here when

*"... a surprising sight among the blur of masts"*

moored in St Just Pool between 1866 and 1899, and some of the original dockyard buildings became a naval hospital. In the last war, the harbour was used as a base by members of the Free French resistance fighters preparing to sail for France, and by US Navy personnel involved in fitting out Seebees landing craft before the invasion.

Before the harbour was built, Mylor probably consisted of no more than the church, the farm of Lawithick just above which later became a pub, and a small ferry to Greatwood Quay on the other side of the creek.

The church, a surprising sight among the blur of masts, is rather lovely; it has a wonderful Norman doorway in the north wall, decorated with a serpent, and a huge granite cross outside the south porch, seven feet of which is buried underground. Inside you can buy a good little guidebook to the church and its chaotic graveyard.

## Restronguet Creek

Nowadays few boats venture much further up than the Pandora Inn at Restronguet Passage, for this creek has suffered more than any other from

63

silting during Cornwall's mining boom. According to H. Michell Whitley, writing in 1881, the Carnon Creek, as it is also known, used to be tidal as far as above Bissoe Bridge (a good four miles above the Pandora), and a map of 1695 shows three-masted barques riding at anchor in Perranwell Creek. Perranwharf, on the creek below, was a major industrial site and river port serving the great mining area nearby, and the Norway Inn recalls the days of the Norwegian timber ships which brought the huge baulks for the mines. Today just feet from the roar of the A39, there is nonetheless a muffled silence enclosing this derelict waterway with its succession of old bearded quays and wharfs.

In the first half of the 19th century, during the peak of mining activity, the river was silting up at the rate of one foot every five years. The Carnon River drains the Gwennap–St Day mining area, at that time the richest and most productive in Cornwall. Restronguet Creek was further distorted and disturbed by at least three attempts to mine the tin deposits beneath the river. The ruined engine house at the entrance to Tallack's Creek, on the north bank, is all that remains of one of these attempts, the Upper Carnon Mine, worked from 1822 to 1827.

## THE PANDORA INN

Deservedly one of Cornwall's most popular pubs, the Pandora Inn began as a passage house serving the ferry crossing from here to Restronguet Point. This ferry was mentioned as early as 1468; it was on the route of the old pack road from Penryn to Truro which remained one of the main roads in the area until the opening of the Truro turnpike in 1828. Beer barrels for the pub used to come over on the ferry because Restronguet Hill was too steep for the drays. In 1791 the ferry actually sank when a horse became over-excited, and several people were drowned, but the crossing continued to be used until 1960 when it ceased regular service due to decline in demand.

The Pandora, which used to be called the Passage House and then the Ship Inn, was renamed in honour of the ship sent to find the *Bounty* mutineers which sank on the Great Barrier Reef in 1791.

## Point, Penpol and Devoran

Point, Penpol and Devoran (a mile upriver) all grew up in the early 19th century, a period of great prosperity in Cornwall. An explosion of activity in the mining fields west of Truro led to a huge trade in imported coal, timber, bricks and lime, and exports of tin and copper ore. There were quays the whole way down the western bank of Penpol Creek—Daniell's Quay at the creek mouth, Lemon Quay and Smelting House Quay—which could be reached by vessels of over 160 tons.

Point remained the principal shipping place on Restronguet Creek until the building of Devoran's wharves in the 1840s. There was also a successful shipbuilding business here, tin and lead smelting works and a tide mill at the creek head (part of the embankment still remains), and yet these villages now have almost nothing to show for it because they have been subjected to such unbridled housing development that the few old cottages left look out of place and embarrassed to be seen here.

In contrast, Devoran is full of charm and interest, despite the tragic and tasteless buildings on the old wharf area. Devoran's short but glorious career as one of Cornwall's busiest ports began with the construction of the Redruth & Chasewater Railway in 1824 which linked the embryonic port with the richest copper mines. There are few indications of this line to be found in Devoran today, but one of the level crossing gates survives by the side of the main Truro to Falmouth road, and the section from Devoran to Point which was always worked by horses, even after the rest of the line employed locomotives, is now a minor road hugging the riverbank all the way to Point.

The construction of Devoran's docks began in 1838, and later maps show a chaotic system of dykes, channels, wharfs and quays along the riverbank linked by hundreds of sidings spread out like feathery fingers from the spur lines of the railway. The port flourished, yet only 30 years after the completion of the docks Devoran's flame was already guttering due to the failure of the Gwennap mines.

Down on Narabo Quay today, by the massive granite mooring bollards and the rank of ruined ore bins, where once the railway trucks on a raised wooden trestle behind tipped their loads of copper ore to await shipment, there is that strange post-industrial silence, broken only by the distant roar of traffic crossing over the Devoran embankment.

## Pill Creek

The entrance to the slither of water called Pill Creek is tree-hung, rocky and exciting, and once inside you should be in the middle of nowhere, but instead you are in the middle of Feock. The atmosphere in this secretive gorge, which has been so comprehensively embraced by an affluent village, is oppressive. There are still some fine old cottages near the water's edge, but you can barely see them for the chains and barriers and 'Private' signs.

The main quay at Pill is along the eastern bank of the creek; it is still a solid and impressive structure, although of little use these days. It was built in 1765 to encourage the development of Pill as a port for the mines, and for some time this little place thrived. The trade in copper ore declined after 1827 in favour of Point which by then had a railway link with the mines. Transport down to Pill by packhorse had always been slow and hazardous. Shipbuilding still carried on here, however, mostly under the Ferris family who also built at Point, and many of the early oyster dredgers—the Falmouth working boats—were built on Pill's quays.

## THE OYSTER FISHERY

This northern half of the Carrick Roads is where the main oyster beds are to be found, and there are strict controls on the working of them. The season lasts from October 1 to March 31, and the beds are dredged under sail only by the distinctive working boats. There is a working core of about fifteen of these boats which may rise to as many as 40 in a profitable season. This is the last working sailing fleet in Western Europe and a focus of much local pride and interest. The design of individual boats varies considerably, as boatbuilders all over Cornwall used to experiment and adapt constantly to suit different conditions and requirements. Many are now used for pleasure only, and they are raced very competitively.

### The River Fal

The Fal proper begins beyond Turnaware Point, from where many Americans set sail for the beaches of Normandy in 1944, and Channals Creek, with the great house of Trelissick above gazing down the Carrick Roads to the sea. The gardens at Trelissick are owned by the National Trust and open to the public from March to the end of October, with a woodland walk open for the rest of the year.

The entrance to the Fal makes a glorious contrast with the grand chasm of the Carrick Roads, being secret and narrow and darkly wooded. Largely due to the good management of the Tregothnan Estate, the Fal is how all Cornish rivers should be—completely undeveloped and copiously clad in deciduous forest. Much of the forest is oak coppice, the bark from which still goes to the tannery at Grampound as it has done for centuries.

The Fal's natural beauty is emphasized rather than impaired by the presence of the huge ships waiting for employment or idling away their last years in the quiet deep water above King Harry Ferry. These rusting giants have nowhere to go and nothing to do; they are bitter reminders of the speed at which Britain's merchant fleet is shrinking. The laying-up of ships on the Fal is by no means a new thing. In the 1930s the reaches above Turnaware were heavily used by tramp steamers, and since then there have been liners, tankers and freighters here most of the time—as many as thirty during trade depressions. Many were and are under foreign registry. After the last war, in particular, there were a great many unwanted ships about, a good number of which found their way into the Fal causing terrible congestion.

## KING HARRY FERRY AND TOLVERNE

The Ferry is one of Cornwall's ancient river crossings on the old coastal route through the county. A sturdy chain ferry runs here today, but as late as 1887 there was still a simple boat rowed across by one or two men. At that time the possibility of building a high-level bridge instead was being discussed, because the crossing was so hazardous in bad weather that travellers had to make a 20 mile detour through Truro and Tregony. Two

*'the Fal's natural beauty is emphasized . . .*
*by the presence of the huge ships waiting for employment'*

years later, however, the rowing boat was replaced by a larger, steadier steam ferry.

On the west bank there used to be an inn, King Henry's Passage House, in one of the joined cottages facing the ferry; with such a position, what a shame that it is no more. On the opposite shore, up on the hill, there once stood a chapel dedicated to St Mary, but by 1528 the name had been changed to 'Our Lady and King Henry'. The Henry in question, and thus the Harry of the passage, was King Henry VI who had had a couple of fairly disastrous reigns in the previous century, and who was now being put up for canonization in Rome some 50 years after his death. The campaign was unsuccessful, but it led to his name being added to the chapel's dedication and thus immortalized in the name of a Cornish river crossing.

Just beyond King Harry Ferry, on the corner as the river turns to the right, perches the so-called Smuggler's Cottage of Tolverne. This unbelievably quaint, toffee-tin cottage, now a restaurant, is about 500 years old, the oldest part being the wing to the rear. What extraordinary scenes there must have been here during the build-up to D-Day, when this place, like Turnaware, was one of the main embarkation points for American troops. The road down here and the beach in front of the cottage were both especially made so that landing barges could pick up troops and material, and a pier was built out across two-thirds of the river.

67

Eisenhower, the Supreme Commander of the Allied Forces, actually came to this bemused little cottage in the midst of Jeeps and concrete and camouflage in order to meet top members of his command. There used to be a passenger ferry, which died from lack of use, from Tolverne across to Halwyn, in Kea, where an old green lane still runs down to the shore.

## Lamouth Creek and Cowlands Creek

*ROUNDWOOD*

Opposite Tolverne are the shallow, silted creeks of Lamouth and Cowlands, with Roundwood Quay between them. The sturdy wharves, now protected by the National Trust, owe their existence to the enterprising Daniell family who also developed Point and Pill. This was for some time a major shipping place for tin and copper ore, and in 1798 it was noted that vessels of 300 tons could moor alongside the quays on even the lowest of tides.

As a mining port Roundwood did not last long; like Pill, it suffered from the building of the Redruth & Chasewater Railway to Devoran and Point. Roundwood was too far from the mines for packhorse transport to be economic; the rough old track down to the quays from the road, still the only land route here, gives you some idea of how the roads would have been for the entire journey. Despite losing the ore trade, Roundwood continued to be quite a centre of industry. From 1861 to 1877 the celebrated shipbuilder H. S. Trethowan, of Bar Pool and Little Falmouth, had a yard here, and his success encouraged a number of others to set up in business, as the unusual number of launching slipways around the quays suggests.

On the wooded hill above Roundwood Quay lurk the remains of an ancient hill fort, so this might have been a trading port back in the Iron Age. Rounds and encampments such as this one are normally to be found in the open; there is something sinister about those which have been masked in woodland, so that their great embankments come looming indistinctly and suddenly out of the undergrowth.

Lamouth Creek, owned by the National Trust, is on the south side of Roundwood and one of the most peaceful places imaginable. Cowlands Creek, the name coming from kew-nans, 'a ravine', (Lamouth's name means 'valley of the pigs'), is a rare example of a creek which is lived in but not spoiled. There are one or two blots in Cowlands itself, at the creek head, but the hamlet of Coombe is a dream. This is all Tregothnan land, and there can be no doubt that had Lord Falmouth not owned it Coombe would by now be a Point or Penpoll, or worse, being so close to Truro, and there would be a marina in deep water nearby.

A footpath leads right along the north bank of the creek from Cowlands to Halwyn (a place of the strangest atmosphere) past the orchards, some forgotten now, which produce the famous Kea Plums.

*Roundwood Quay—'. . . a major shipping place for tin and copper ore'*

## Old Kea

Beyond the fork in the river where the Fal heads off to the east, and past the old quays and boathouses of Tregothnan (the huge house on the hill above can be seen from down near Tolverne), the church tower of Old Kea peeps out from near the willowy head of a tiny creek. This desolate tower is all that remains of what was once the mother church of a 7000 acre parish. The church was inconveniently placed at the outer edge of the parish, and as early as the 16th century parishioners were asking for a new, more central one. They finally received it in 1802, when All Hallows Church was built about three miles inland, and then all but the 15th century tower of the old church was demolished. This is an ancient holy site; a Celtic monastery was founded here by the Irish St Kea, and the strangely marked stone outside the small replacement church (built for £111 in the shadow of the tower), is probably a relic of this 5th century foundation.

## Malpas

The name Malpas means, in Norman-French, 'the treacherous crossing'. A two-branched rowing ferry, linking St Michael Penkevil on the east

69

*'a two-branched rowing ferry . . . has long since replaced the ancient ford'*

with Malpas and Kea, has long since replaced the ancient ford here, and the ferryman's cottage on the St Michael Penkevil bank must rate as one of the loveliest houses on the river. In the early 1800s the ferry was run by the infamous 'Mopus Jenny', whose real name was Jane Davies. In 1804 she singlehandedly rescued Lord Falmouth's stolen mail, as well as rounding up the robbers into the bargain. When asked what generally caused her the most trouble in crossing the river, she would reputedly answer 'Wemmen and pigs!' The old ferry landing on the Kea bank can be reached by a green lane which runs from the Woodbury Road down through the woods (a protected heronry) to the river. This is a peaceful, lonely spot from which to appreciate the bustle of Malpas, in particular the hollow hammering from the boatyards which leaps across the water and echoes back from the wooded hills all about.

The old ford at Malpas figures largely in the famous legend of Tristan and Iseult, as it is told by the 12th century poet Béroul. The ford is actually mentioned three times: in the third instance Iseult, having left her lover Tristan and returned to her husband King Mark, is being taken by Mark to his manor of 'Blancheland' (Goodern in Kea) where she will have to swear that she has always been faithful to him. She secretly arranges for Tristan to meet the royal party at 'Le Mal Pas', disguised as a leper, and for him to offer to carry her across the ford. In so doing, he stumbled and fell to the ground with her; she was thus able to swear at Blancheland that she had never lain with any man but her husband and that leper who fell with her at the ford—a pretty clever trick by anyone's standards.

The 'forest of Morois' where Béroul says the lovers had been hiding before Iseult's return to Mark, has been identified with the manor of Moresk which, in the Domesday Book, owned the largest amount of woodland in West Cornwall, of which the wooded banks of the Truro and Tresillian Rivers are just the remaining fragments.

## THE VILLAGE

The popular Heron Inn, with its wonderful view down the Truro River, is called after the heronry in the woods opposite. It used to be the Park Inn after Park Farm which lies about half a mile inland and which used to own the whole of Malpas, along with all the land between Bar Creek just to the north of the village and the outskirts of Truro where the police station is now. In the second half of the 18th century a solicitor called Charles Warrick lived at Park Farm. No ordinary man of law, he invented the paddle, as later used in paddle steamers; his was hand-driven, mounted on a crank, and he used it to propel himself up and down the river to Truro and back. It must have been quite a sight.

In the past, Malpas was famous both for oysters (which gradually became infected by copper waste) and shipbuilding. In the 1880s, the celebrated yard of Scoble & Davies built the largest ship to be constructed in the port of Truro, the 180 ton three-masted *Malpas Belle*, which went on to become the only Truro vessel ever to round Cape Horn.

In 1846 Queen Victoria and Prince Albert sailed up to Malpas in the royal yacht during their seaborne tour of the South Coast. They anchored just off what was then called Downe's Point, since renamed Victoria Point, and there the Queen remained while her husband went upriver to visit Truro.

## The River up to Truro

This section of the river suffered from its fair share of silting in the last century, although not to the extent of Restronguet Creek. Calenick Creek, to the left opposite Sunny Corner, was particularly badly choked by mining waste, however, and what was once a lively waterway for barges and lighters is now just a muffled inlet.

Although Truro's position as one of Cornwall's leading ports was badly hit by the development of Falmouth, mining imports and exports kept the place alive. There was actually a big increase in the amount of tin exported through Truro (nearly half the county's tin exports) in the second half of the 17th century, just when Falmouth was becoming a threat in general trade. In the next two centuries the vigorous development of mining west of Truro ensured that this port continued to be the chief outlet for tin and copper ore, despite competition from Calenick, Pill, Roundwood, Point, Devoran, Perranwharf and Penryn.

The Newham Quay area, still a thriving trading centre on the left going up to Truro, was built up in the last century and served by a branch railway from 1855. Newham actually served as Truro's sole station until the Cornwall Railway arrived from the east, to join up with the West Cornwall Railway in 1859, and the present station site came into use. The line of the old Newham railway is still clearly visible.

The old quayside areas, which fringe the river as it now idles into the heart of the city, formed the nursery of Truro's commerce and industry; many have slumbered, neglected, for almost a hundred years but are now experiencing a reversal of their fortunes. Where this has meant the re-employment of old warehouses by small businesses, it can only be good for the waterfront, but the large-scale inappropriate development of vacant sites by superstores is less welcome.

What is particularly heartening about the new businesses on Truro's and Newham's quays is that not all of them have turned away from the river, dismissing Cornwall's greatest artery of communication which laps at their back doors. Some, such as the Cornish Calcified Seaweed Company on Newham Quay, actually still rely on the river for their livelihood. This thriving little business dredges up calcified seaweed (a great source of calcium, magnesium and other minerals and trace elements, thus a vital fertilizer) from the bed of the Carrick Roads, and the load is then barged upriver to Newham for grading, draining and drying. This is a successful revival of an ancient Cornish industry; in 1662, for instance, John Ray wrote of Truro: 'Here is an indifferent good quay. They dredge up from the bottom of the sea abundance of a sort of white coral, among the sand, wherewith they manure their land'.

## Truro

Cornwall's capital city is Truro, a wonderful place which is dominated by the cathedral 'riding like a full-rigged vessel above the sunken city' (J. C. Trewin). Although the town centre occasionally changes for the worse, Truro has yet to succumb to the epidemic of uniformity. It has a unique and very Cornish atmosphere which comes from a strange mixture: its origins as a port on the confluence of the Rivers Allen and Kenwyn, together with its development as both a rural market town and a place of Georgian fashion and elegance. It is a winning combination.

Two things, above all else, should not be missed in Truro. One is the County Museum in River Street—small and fascinating and home to Lamorna Birch's 'Morning Fills the Bowl' and other fine Cornish paintings; it also deals extensively with the mining and other industries, and archaeological finds. The other essential is the cathedral, which was built for Cornwall between 1880 and 1910. Some people still do not like it, though it is hard to imagine why. Somehow it feels absolutely right: it is Cornwall's cathedral in the way it rises up out of the city and yet is jumbled in with the shops and houses; in the way it does not distance itself, in the sanctity of a close, from the grubby, secular aspects of urban life but is always right there—you bump into it when emerging from the Post Office or Littlewoods. This accessibility is largely due to the cathedral being built so late, long after the town had already grown up and filled in, and also to the fact that it incorporates part of the 16th century parish church

*'. . . the nursery of Truro's commerce and industry'*

of St Mary, which is why, perhaps, it has the atmosphere of being Truro's parish church more than its cathedral. The difficulty of squeezing a new cathedral into the middle of a flourishing town is perfectly illustrated by the view from the west door (the one by the Post Office) down towards the altar; it is quite clear from this angle that the building is bent.

## The Tresillian River

Until the 1930s, the river was busy with ketches, schooners and barges bringing in grain for the maltings (the strangely shaped building still exists, beside the main road) along with roadstone, coal and timber to the quays at Tresillian, at the head of the creek. As with all the other creeks, this one is not as navigable now as it was in the past, and the village of Tresillian, being on a major road, does not need the river any longer. The road has also meant that Tresillian has developed from a knot of cottages around the bridge, and a pub nearer the quays, into a noisy, strung-out and unattractive village.

The river itself has a certain shabby grandeur, and is followed on both sides by once-elegant carriageways. The one on the east bank is the four mile long private drive to Tregothnan, but the western one from St Clement to Tresillian is a public right of way and a lovely, gentle walk. It is the 'under-road' of W. P. Hodgkinson's memorable description:

'To me there is a magic in the changing Cornish scene, which can best be sensed inland—particularly among the wooded valleys of the Fal and Helford Rivers. There is just such a magic about the Under-Road as it leaves the beautiful village of St Clement and passes beneath the lichen-fragrant trees at the edge of the creek. On the way, one gets an occasional peep of the creek and its mud-banks, clothed right down to the water's edge with thick woodland. Half a mile beyond, the road passes a large pond upon which the alert birdwatcher may see anything from a spoonbill to a dabchick, according to the season of the year. And when the tide is in, having the appearance of a tranquil lake, or low—so that it is a mere brook between the steep mud banks—the "ebbers" will be out with their ebbing-nets, standing like lone sentinels in their boats.'

In the summer of 1986 a new riverbank footpath was created by five working parties from the British Trust for Conservation Volunteers, to link St Clement with Malpas, so that for the first time the whole tidal length of the Tresillian River can be walked. Branching off this new footpath at one point, and heading up through the woods into the open hills high above the river, there is an ancient green lane called Dennis Lane, from 'dynas' meaning a fort. In a field just to the south of it, the ruined walls of a 19th century barn are said to mark the approximate site of Moresk Castle, the nucleus of the ancient and important manor of Moresk which is supposed to have been destroyed in the early 12th century.

The village of St Clement is astonishingly unspoilt, and its position idyllic. Nestling outside the churchyard there is an almost unbearably pretty little square of cottages, along with a slate-faced lych gate which in the past has served as parish vestry room, village school, Sunday school and pigsty.

## The Upper Fal

The last tidal part of the Fal, barely navigable now, which idles up from Tregothnan boathouse towards Ruan Lanihorne, must be one of the most peaceful stretches of water on earth. Here, the fingers of the sea are reaching deep into the remote, agricultural folds of inland Cornwall.

Ardevora Point juts out into the river to such an extent that it appears to form two lakes, one on its upstream and one on its downstream side. The Rev. John Whitaker who wrote, among other things, a history of Ruan Lanihorne in the late 18th century, used to call the quiet and sedgy upstream lake 'Little Falmouth Harbour' or 'Ruan Bay'. On the left bank of Ruan Bay, in a lonely inlet, is the churchtown of Lamorran. Tiny and unspoilt, the church and hamlet are not generous with their charms; the church is kept locked and you cannot wander happily around the inlet or down to the shores of the Fal because everything is feudally private.

The right bank of Ruan Bay is dominated by the solitary chimney of what used to be the Trelonk Brickworks. Bricks fashioned here went to build many of the riverside farms. Oystermen were employed in the off-season to collect faggots of wood from the banks of the Fal to fuel the kilns, and a tramway used to run out from the quay to the river channel so that loading could be carried on at all stages of the tide.

## THE LOST PORT OF TREGONY

The upper Fal is perhaps the most seriously silted of all the creeks on the estuary, although much of the damage was done in a much earlier mining age than that which clogged the Restronguet and Calenick Creeks. Incredibly, the tide used to flow for another three or four miles above Ruan Bay, and Tregony, one of Cornwall's most attractive inland villages, used to be a busy medieval port with 36 alehouses to keep the sailors happy.

In 1584, Norden explained that the sea once brought 'Boates of reasonable burden farr above Tregony . . . but the sea having refused this office of ease to that part of the country, checked (as it seemeth) by the minerall sandes which fall into manie places, to the prejudice of the havens, leaveth the inhabitants to a more ircksome cariage of their sundrie necessaries'.

## RUAN LANIHORNE

As Tregony declined so Ruan Lanihorne flourished, and as early as the 14th century it appeared in a list of Cornish ports as 'Lanihorne', along with the likes of Truro, Penryn and St Mawes. In time, however, it also began to suffer from the same curse. The silting was made much worse in the last century by the discovery of china clay further up the Fal, and now it is almost as hard to imagine Ruan Lanihorne as a port as it is Tregony.

Hockin, who considered Ruan Lanihorne to be 'the most perfect of creek-side villages', gave to this lonely place one of his most memorable descriptions: 'An intense and unassailable peace lies between the thick roll of the Lamorran woods and the drowsy curve of the meadowed Roseland shore . . . and the lazy tide comes seeping soundlessly over the mud through long, level strips of rush-fledged marsh to the old village.' Despite some aggressively placed new housing, the village is still charming and has a good little pub called the King's Head. The church is wonderful: stout, stumpy and rubble-built with ivy and creepers ranging in abandon over the walls, it has an air of dignified dilapidation.

The most extraordinary thing about Ruan Lanihorne is that there used to be here an important 'castle of a 7 toures', as Leland described it. From its first mention in the early 14th century to the reign of Henry VII it was considered to have been the largest and finest castle, with the exception of Launceston, in the whole county. It was situated somewhere down by the creek on the lower road, somewhere amongst the families of geese, the rusting cars and bits of farm machinery, and the tumbledown buildings, many of which must incorporate stone from the castle. It seems a strange and claustrophobic place, caught between the swells of two hills, in which to build a castle, but when the river was navigable and Ruan was a port there must have been a different atmosphere here altogether.

## St Just-in-Roseland

This church is Cornwall's Taj Mahal: it is over-visited and over-photographed, you are sure it will be a disappointment, but it will exceed your expectations. John Betjeman wrote in the *Shell Guide to Cornwall* that it is 'to many people the most beautiful churchyard on earth'; that is quite a reputation to live up to.

Jack Clemo, the famous blind poet of the china clay country, has caught the elusive spirit of St Just:

> Roots of bamboo, eucalyptus, palm,
> Curl towards buried Cornish saints;
> Exotic leaves twang a jungle prayer
> Above the river-bed now drained at ebb-tide,
> Where boats lounge on mud-banks and wait
> For the gurgling inwash from Falmouth Bay.

If the churchyard has a few too many tarmacadam paths and picnic tables, it also has the constant susurrus of rooks and running water, a holy well among the weeping willows, monkey puzzles and stands of bamboo, weed-choked ponds, palm trees right up to the church walls, a great spread of giant rhubarb, and two old lychgates, the lower one with its Cornish granite cattlegrid intact. Even in the bleakest February drizzle this is still a magical place. Quite apart from the churchyard, there is still the glory of an old Cornish church by tidal water.

The church hides around the corner from the Carrick Roads, boats sprawling on the shingle bar which separates its private inlet from St Just Creek. There used to be a fleet of fishing boats here, mostly oyster dredgers; the yard which repaired and built the working boats now survives on the care of pleasure craft.

### *ST JUST POOL*

There have been several attempts over the years to effect a change at St Just-in-Roseland; none, so far, successful. During the 18th century there was a plan, strongly supported by the influential Admiral Boscawen, to build a naval dockyard in the deep waters of St Just Pool at the mouth of the creek, but Devonport was eventually chosen instead. The Pool continued to be used as a quarantine anchorage for Falmouth Harbour, and as a mooring for naval ships waiting for repairs at Mylor Dockyard. In this century there was a proposal to build wharfs and repair yards in the Pool and create a commercial port. St Just was saved by its isolation from the main road and rail networks. Things would thus have been very different had local squire John Penhallow Peters had his way in the 1830s. His plan was to build a railway linking St Just with Burngullow, which is on the

*'". . . Exotic leaves twang a jungle prayer . . ."'*

main line just west of St Austell, for 'the cheap conveyance of lime, manure etc., to improve agriculture in the Roseland, to reclaim the moors along the Fal, to supply iron, coal and groceries cheaply in the Roseland . . .' The scheme failed, strangely enough, because of the opposition of landowners in the Tregony area.

## St Mawes

Though St Mawes is perhaps the most changed of all the old Cornish fishing villages, the wholehearted discovery of its charms, and its transformation into a sophisticated watering place, did not come about until early in this century. It must have been its glorious position, curled around the sunny south-facing bay at the mouth of the Percuil River, which attracted the attention of the leisured classes because the town itself is usually spoken of in disparaging terms.

Until 1832 St Mawes had been a parliamentary borough ('more by favour than by merit', Carew observed drily), but after its disenfranchisement the town's patron the Marquis of Buckingham lost interest and on May 13, 1842 the whole place was up for sale.

Things were obviously looking up by 1854, however, when a new sea wall and approach road were about to be built and the pier and quay reconstructed. The pier, now listed, which took nearly twenty years to rebuild, is of unknown age; Leland noted it in 1539, but it is probably considerably older, and was the most important structure in the medieval fishing and trading port.

To find the remnants of that old fishing village, you will need to slip up one of the side streets that climb the hill away from the harbour, for the waterfront is now almost entirely changed. St Mawes has become a place of good hotels and restaurants (the Rising Sun is highly thought of), up-market gift shops, delicatessens, boutiques and fudge shops, where it is strangely difficult to buy a pasty.

## TO THE CASTLE AND BEYOND

The road up to the castle runs past Tavern Beach, so called because there used to be a pub here where the St Mawes men on the lookout for piloting work used to gather, scanning the horizon for an approaching ship. Before regulations and licences were brought in in 1808, anyone with local knowledge could have a go, and pilotage in the Fal estuary became the special reserve of St Mawes sailors and fishermen.

The history of St Mawes Castle, the clover-leaf castle, is ironic: although stoutly built on the tip of its peninsula and superbly positioned to protect St Mawes and the Carrick Roads from French and Spanish attacks (in just 40 years before it was built, St Mawes was raided at least twice), the castle nevertheless failed the only serious test in its entire history. It was not built for, and did not expect, a civil war—how could anyone have anticipated, a century beforehand, that Englishmen would be killing each other on the battlefield? Pendennis, on an ancient fortified site, was strong by land as well as by water, but St Mawes was impossible to defend from the landward side and the governor of the castle during the war, Hannibal Bonython, had no choice but to surrender to General Fairfax of the Parliamentary Army in March 1646.

St Mawes Castle has never really been allowed to recover from the ignominy of that capitulation, and sometimes it has even been made a figure of fun; Byron for instance wrote that 'Pendennis they will not let us behold, save at a distance, because Hobhouse and I are suspected of having already taken St Mawes by a *coup de main*'.

Beyond the castle a footpath leads along the unspoilt shore of the Carrick Roads, beneath the tousled gorse, bracken and blackthorn of the National Trust's Newton Cliff, to St Just-in-Roseland. This eastern part of the Carrick Roads, as far south as St Anthony Head, along with St Just Creek and the Percuil River, has been designated a voluntary marine conservation area in order to encourage awareness of the importance and sensitivity of the underwater wildlife here. Just off this stretch of coast between St Mawes and St Just lies the St Mawes Bank which contains a large area of eel grass (zostera) supporting many species of fish, worms, molluscs, anemones and hermit crabs, as well as extensive beds of living calcified seaweed or maerl—the only known beds in Southern Britain. It is the dead deposits of this which are dredged up to be used as fertilizer.

About halfway along the path to St Just, just where a stream gushes down the hillside and into a tiny sandy cove, is the site of a pub called the White House of which nothing now remains. Along with the pub itself, in

1766 when it was advertised to let, there was a malt house, a brewing house, a limekiln and a quay, because the majority of the customers would have been seaborne.

## POLVARTH

The Freshwater Boatyard at Polvarth, just up the Percuil River from St Mawes, was made famous by the Peters family from 1790 onwards: they built a variety of working boats and punts, but are celebrated chiefly for their pilot gigs. These slim, six-oared 30 foot clinker-built boats were originally intended to carry pilots out to incoming vessels, but they also became used for salvage work and as early lifeboats. They were especially popular in the Isles of Scilly, providing links between the islands, and gig races are still held in the islands every summer. Other yards may have built them from time to time, but for 100 years the pilot gigs from the Peters' Yard were the best.

## TRETHEM AND POLINGEY

A National Trust footpath runs from the old river port of Percuil around the river shore towards Polingey Creek, and all along the way the Trust has been doing some vital replanting. Already there is a varied and colourful collection of trees sprouting up among the bracken. Along the ridge above the footpath runs the old road from Gerrans down to Percuil, skirting the hill called Dinnies, which comes from 'dynas' suggesting that there used to be a fort or encampment guarding the old crossing from Percuil to the West bank.

From this road the view over the two creeks of Trethem and Polingey is breathtaking. This is a real Roseland view, characterized by its remoteness (the creeks are not really accessible by land); a rumpled eiderdown landscape of hills and fields with little patches of trees, blackthorn and gorse, and the slinky waters in between. The fields here are actually green—not the agonizing yellow of oil seed rape, nor the corrugated white of plastic strawberry guards. The name Roseland comes from the Cornish 'ros' meaning 'promontory' and refers to the district from St Anthony up towards Tregony and extending to Veryan on the east. The Roseland has traditionally been mutton and barley country, but agribusiness is making inroads even here: in places the land use is slowly changing to, for instance, the large scale production of flowers.

Both Trethem and Polingey Creeks used to have watermills at their upper ends. Trethem Mill, powered by an overshot wheel, was the oldest of the Percuil River mills, and the one at Polingey (the name means millhouse) was a tide mill driven by the release of water from a man-made pool at the creek head.

## St Anthony-in-Roseland

At the head of Porth (also known as Froe) Creek there used to be another tide mill, of which the embankment and pool are still in good order. In the early years of this century coal was still being landed from small sailing craft at the head of this creek, but the mill stopped grinding in the 19th century.

The land between the head waters of Porth Creek and the sea at Towan Beach is narrow, low and shingly, and many people believe that St Anthony was once an island. There is certainly a strange and insular atmosphere here; it can become quite claustrophobic as streams of visitors' cars are funnelled in along the one road towards the car park on St Anthony Head. The view from the Head is outstanding, and there is the added attraction of the Georgian lighthouse below (beacon fires were lit on the headland for centuries before it was built), but there are also other less crowded places around to be discovered.

### THE CHURCH

The greatest destination of all in this island parish is the church of St Anthony which cowers behind the extraordinary pile of Place House; church and house are actually joined. As you walk down the church path there is no prior warning of the churchyard: you just come upon gravestones sprouting out of the undergrowth. It is a glorious riot of granite and slate, and even an open medieval coffin, among bluebells and nettles and docks.

The little cruciform church itself really is lovely. Although it was comprehensively restored in 1850, Pevsner still considers it to be 'the best example in the county of what a parish church was like in the 12th and 13th centuries'. There is a magnificent Norman doorway; and inside, the cool tiled floor and the bright stained glass scattering coloured light about in the semidarkness give it the simple atmosphere of a French mountain chapel.

### PLACE

The reason for the rather insolent position of Place House is that it occupies the site of a monastery which had existed until the Reformation in the early 16th century, despite being burned down once by French pirates in 1338. The lawn of Place now covers most of the old pool of the monks' tide mill.

A rowing ferry to St Mawes used to serve the village of Bohortha on the hill above, as well as Place, and a footpath which emerges down near the slipway linked the old village with the quay and the ferry landing. There are several good walks around here: one goes up alongside the Percuil River and then up Porth Creek, clinging to the shoreline all the way; another sets off in the other direction, halfway around Cellars Beach (the enchanting cottages are built on the foundations of 17th century fish cellars), then across the hill to the coast and on to St Anthony Head.

*Gorran Haven—'the most eloquent of waterfronts'*

# 5   From St Anthony Head to St Austell Bay

| 1880 | 1960 |
|---|---|
| Peaceful little land-locked harbour, | Bed and breakfast. Bed and breakfast. |
| Fish-nets drying in the sun, | Bed and breakfast. Fish and chips. |
| Placid house-wives knitting guernseys | Ices. Films. Live bait. NO PARKING. |
| After-dinner duties done. | Bus timetables. Coaching trips. |
| Fishers snatch an hour's siesta, | Picture postcards. Pasties. Pixies. |
| Cats asleep on window-sills, | Petrol. Car Park. Traffic jam. |
| Children at their board-school lessons, | 'Quaint old Cornish fishing village? |
| Tranquil lie the enfolding hills. | Let's get back to Birmingham!' |

Frank Baron, 'Mevagissey Past and Present'
from *Mevagissey Backalong*

THE harbours which pierce the lonely coastline between St Anthony Head and St Austell Bay fall roughly into two categories: the ancient, gritty fishing harbours, some with only tiny breakwaters and minimal shelter; and the planned industrial harbours, built in the early 19th century to serve the booming mining area around St Austell. Of the three planned harbours, only Charlestown can still be visited by private craft, and of the fishing ports only Mevagissey shows signs of ever having flourished, with a large outer as well as an inner harbour and a surviving fishing fleet.

## Portscatho

Tucked in on the eastern shore of lovely Gerrans Bay is the bleak and open village of Portscatho. Do not be put off by the seafront which is bland and ugly: behind it there is a charming square, a good pub (the oldest building in the village, it is claimed) and some interesting little shops. The heart of the village, the atmosphere of the place, is right, so it does not really matter that Portscatho is not as pretty from the water as Portloe or Mousehole.

Portscatho's Cornish name means the 'harbour of large boats', and for many hundreds of unrecorded years fishing boats have used what little natural shelter they could find here to carry on their modest and unspectacular business. The little pier, which looks strangely out of place, has a rather curious history which began in the Great Blizzard of 1891. Along with many other Cornish harbours, Portscatho received quite a battering, as the *Royal Cornwall Gazette* of March 19 reported: 'In addition to the terrible wreck in house property, several quays are washed down as well as the coastguard's watch and boathouse, the boat itself having a narrow escape. Several craft were washed away from the quays and smashed to atoms.' As well, a German ship, the 900 ton *Carl Hirschberg* on her way from Hamburg to Cardiff, was driven ashore amidst the rocks that gave the fishing cove some natural shelter. She lay there, stuck fast, for a month, during which time the villagers put up the crew in their own homes. At last the Board of Trade gave permission for the rocks imprisoning her to be dynamited, on condition that an artificial breakwater be built to replace them. *Black's Guide* of 1911 commented that this new pier was 'not so effectual a breakwater as Nature's own'.

In 1869 the people of Portscatho fought hard to get the proposed new lifeboat station, which was to provide intermediate cover between Mevagissey and Falmouth, sited in their harbour. The rival site, which had some influential backers, was Portloe. A correspondent asserted in the *Royal Cornwall Gazette* that at Portscatho there was 'plenty of searoom both right and left' and went on to write that, 'I would challenge the whole Lifeboat Institution to find a worse place than Portloe, or a better place than Portscatha, for a lifeboat station'. Portloe, a tiny gap in the cliffs of Veryan Bay beyond Nare Head, was eventually chosen, but time was to prove the advocates of Portscatho right.

## Portloe

Great black curtains of rock are drawn almost completely across the entrance to the fishing cove of Portloe; it is practically impossible to get in or out in bad weather. The original lifeboat house stood just opposite where the road goes down to the beach. To launch, the boat had to be drawn out of its house on to the road, broadside-on to the hill, then swivelled around and let down the steep slope to the beach. On one occasion, during a practice session, she ran away out of control and crashed into a shop. A new house and slip was then built up against the

*'its situation is cramped and dramatic . . .'*

cliff on the beach. The old house became an Anglican church and a chancel was added to it, while the new one was converted to the village school after the lifeboat station closed in 1887. The Portloe station lasted for seventeen years and in that time performed not a single service—due to a combination of lack of suitable opportunities and the difficulties in launching the boat and getting out of the cove.

Portloe is undoubtedly one of the loveliest of all the fishing harbours; its situation is cramped and dramatic, and it has neither an ugly sea-face nor an ugly heart. It has a little salt-swept hotel right down by the beach (the car park of which is on the site of the old pilchard cellars), a fine set of limekilns up above, squashed unceremoniously into a row of cottages, and an extraordinary lack of the inappropriate buildings now normally found in Cornwall's delightful places. The most atmospheric description of the place comes from Harper's *The Cornish Coast*, in 1910: 'Portloe is a gloomy inlet amid dark overhanging cliffs. Down there is the poor fishing village, in a primitive state, absolutely untouched by pleasure-seekers, and apparently not thriving in its fishery. But its situation down there, below the echoing cliffs reverberating to the mocking cries of the sea gulls, is magnificent.'

It is ironic that one of the main reasons why Portloe beat Portscatho for the lifeboat station was that the latter was said to have a shortage of available men to crew the boat. Today it is Portloe, not Portscatho, which would have the problems. As in so many unspoilt places, the fishermen's cottages here are being bought up as holiday homes at prices no Cornish people can afford. Large stacks of inkwell pots on the slip show that there is still crabbing going on here, a fishery for which Portloe has long been famed (and the Ship Inn is said by some to do the best crab sandwiches in Cornwall); at least there is a working community, even if it is small, but for how much longer? The sad trend is still for the beautiful places like Portloe to degenerate into holiday villages, hollow and deserted for seven months of the year.

## Gorran Haven

The dark bulk of Dodman Point encloses Veryan Bay on the east, and on the far side of it lies Gorran Haven. It is tempting to work up the Cornish coast describing each place in turn as an 'ancient fishing harbour', so that the reader's palate for ancient fishing harbours becomes a little jaded after a time. Of Gorran Haven there is actually no need to say anything at all: the sturdy granite pier shelters the most eloquent of waterfronts with its boat pound, Coastguard boathouse, storehouses and limekilns. Unlike Portscatho, at Gorran Haven the area closest to the water is the best; the further inland you go, the more its charms recede.

One of the earliest known references to seine fishing in Cornwall concerns Gorran Haven: in 1270 Gorran Church (the parish church a mile inland) was given to Glasney College at Penryn, along with the tithe of the seine nets and of all the seine boats in the parish above the number of twelve. The old name of Gorran Haven is Porth-East, the popular explanation being that it was to the east of the Dodman. Cornwall's great historian Charles Henderson has, however, shown it to be a corruption of 'Porth-Just' and the little 15th century chapel in the village is dedicated to St Just. The first small protective pier was built at the same time as the chapel, by the Bodrugans who owned the whole of Gorran Haven and were its guardians and benefactors. The most famous Bodrugan is Sir Henry, who was also the last. Almost alone among Cornish landowners, he supported the Yorkist cause in the Wars of the Roses. After the accession of the Lancastrian Henry Tudor to the throne, Bodrugan's local enemy Sir Richard Edgcumbe was sent to arrest him. Local tradition has it that, on hearing of Edgcumbe's approach, Sir Henry raced, upon his horse, for the cliffs near Chapel Point and leapt off on to a small rock just offshore, where he had a boat waiting to speed him into exile in Ireland. The Edgcumbe family may have won all the Bodrugan lands in the end, but Sir Henry won the fame and immortality: whether or not the story is true, Bodrugan's Leap is now an official place name.

## THE FISHING COMMUNITY

Gorran Haven's progress as a fishing port was unsteady but by the end of the 19th century, after the old pier had been rebuilt by Squire Williams of Caerhays, there were 30 boats and 60 fishermen here, not to mention a flourishing boatbuilding industry. It was said at the time that the boats built here were famous throughout the country, and that many East-countrymen preferred a Gorran boat to one built on the East Coast. Gorran Haven crabpots, woven from withies (willow twigs), were also sold to the fishermen of Devon and Ireland, and it is as a crabbing community that the village has been best known for most of this century.

Never before in its history have Gorran Haven's links with the sea been as tenuous as they are today—there have surely never been fewer villagers whose livelihoods depended on it—but the ghost of the tough little fishing village still walks the changing streets. Nowhere can it be sensed more clearly or more movingly than in the sturdy salty chapel of St Just, which squats without ceremony among the fishermen's cottages above the beach. After the Reformation this little house of God was used as a store (in 1651 it was noted that 'the fishermen made it a house to keepe their sea tackell therein'), and later it was divided into two storeys with the lower half a fish cellar and the upper a Wesleyan chapel. It was restored to its original use in the 1860s. Above the altar, set into the thick sea-facing wall which shrugs off the wildest easterly gales, there is a stained glass window with three sea pictures: Jesus with the fishermen hauling in the nets, Jesus walking on the water, and Jesus and the fishermen safely on the shore with a familiar little haven in the background. The pictures are accompanied by the most evocative of sea verses from the Psalms.

## UP TO THE DODMAN

You can walk to Dodman Point from Gorran Haven either along the coastal path via Maenease Point or Lamledra Farm, or along the unfenced road which takes you high above the great sweep of Vault Beach to Penare, a crouching group of granite buildings that is the Dodman's gatehouse. In a county fringed with forbidding cliffs and headlands, the Dodman (known locally as the 'Deadman') has the most intimidating atmosphere of them all; it steals out to fill you with dread as you pass beneath that dark face in a boat.

A massive earthen bank, stretching right across the headland, is just about all that remains of the Iron Age fortifications which turned the Dodman into a huge cliff castle. Beyond the bank, you walk in high open fields straight out to sea, with the coastline falling back on either side. The Rev. George Martin erected the huge granite cross on the cliff edge in 1896. He spent the night of its dedication, and others subsequently, out on the Dodman praying for shipwrecked souls. Just inland from the cross there is a little building half hidden in the gorse which could be mistaken for a chapel accompanying the cross, surrounded as it is by a low sanctuary wall; it is a 19th century Coastguard hut.

The freakishly rough waters around the Dodman have claimed many lives over the centuries and left many tragedies unexplained. As recently as 1966, 31 people, including seven children, were lost in mysterious circumstances on a 45 foot pleasure cruiser called the *Darlwin*, returning to Mylor from Fowey in the early evening of July 31 in increasingly nasty weather. The search for the lost vessel went on for days over a wide area, and even the Royal Yacht *Brittania* joined in (she happened to be in Devonport for maintenance), but the main body of the wreck and most of the corpses were never found. A Falmouth seaman was reported in the *Cornish Guardian* as saying that he reckoned 'she went down near Dodman Point, where dangerous rocks stretch out to sea just under the surface. On a dirty night like Sunday everybody on board her would have been sheltering in the cabin. She could have hit a reef and gone down like a stone.' Later, a Gorran Haven woman claimed to have noticed the boat out of her kitchen window as she was washing up, and then looked again a few moments later to find it had disappeared. From time to time, even now, Mevagissey fishermen working off the Dodman still trawl up pieces of what they claim to be the wreck of the *Darlwin*.

## Mevagissey

This is a tricky place to describe; it is elusive, secretive and contradictory—Cornish, in fact. In the summer it is the Mevagissey of Frank Baron's glorious poem at the beginning of this chapter (an anthem to all Cornish fishing villages), a popular holiday spot thronged with tourists taking photographs of fishermen, with the old harbourside storehouses obligingly given over to gift shops and ice cream parlours; and yet there is an undercurrent of complete detachment, an insularity that excludes not only tourists but even Cornish people from just up the road. Unless you live in Mevagissey, when you sail into that grand outer harbour or drive down the valley road from behind, you really are entering alien territory.

### FISHING

The most noticeable thing about Mevagissey is that it is still a working town—it has yet to lapse into the role of dormitory town or playground—and in particular a working fishing harbour. It has been so for centuries despite the frequent crises in the industry, like the 1960s when fishing nearly died out altogether here.

Mevagissey's name comes from the two parish saints Meva and Issey or Ida, but the little harbour community itself, as distinct from the parish, used to be called Porthilly. Norden described Porthilly in 1584 as just 'a little fisher village upon the south sea', but by 1824 Stockdale was able to claim that 'as a fisher town, Mevagizzey ranks before any other in the county'.

Mevagissey's first stone pier was built in 1430 and it lasted until the 18th century. A meeting took place in the Ship Inn in February 1774, and an Act of Parliament 'for Completing and maintaining the Pier at Mevagissey' was obtained in November. By 1776 the old pier had been enlarged and a new one added on the western side of the harbour, then in the next ten years further wharves and jetties were built and a regular service of trading vessels was set up between Mevagissey and London. By the mid-19th century there were 80 fishing vessels of all types registered here, giving employment to over 300 fishermen, packers and bulkers and to ten fish-curing businesses, and at the fishery's peak there may have been as many as 20 large pilchard cellars in the village. The large outer harbour which has to bear the brunt of easterly gales was completed in 1890.

In the 1780s the fashionable satirist Peter Pindar, who was born John Wolcot in Fowey, wrote:

> Hail Mevagissey! with such wonders fraught!
> Where boats and men, and stinks, and trade are stirring;
> Where pilchards come in myriads to be caught!
> Pilchards! a thousand times as good as herring.

Myriads of pilchards, indeed myriads of any fish, are a thing of the past, but Mevagissey still has its boats and men, and stinks, and trade, against all the odds. Perhaps this is partly due to an inherent ingenuity among the fishing community here. In the last century, for instance, Mevagissey was at the forefront of experiments in fish-curing at a time when the traditional drysalting (bulking) was just beginning to be seen as laborious and time-consuming. A smokehouse was first built with the object of reviving the old technique of 'fuming', but the smoked pilchards did not meet with popular approval. Then there was 'tanking', the large-scale pickling of pilchards in brine, which was more successful and in which, some say, Mevagissey was a pioneer. The final development was canning in oil, and the pilot scheme for this was certainly launched here.

It has also been suggested that fishing has persisted here because of the particular continuity of Mevagissey people. This is an undiluted society: perhaps that Mevagissey insularity and mistrust of strangers has been fostered over the centuries as a defence against the debilitating influence of foreign blood. Certainly it is not just a newly acquired reaction to the tourist invasion. Even the saintly John Wesley had a few problems here ('Can any good be done in Mevagissey?' he wrote), and there is something strangely familiar about a description by John Taylor (last encountered at St Michael's Mount), who went *Wandering to see the Wonders of the West* in 1649 and found himself in Mevagissey:

'I travelled twelve miles to a fisher town called Mevagissey that Towne hath in it two Tavernes and six Ale-houses, to every one of which I went for lodgings, and not anyone would harbour me; then I sought for a Constable to help me, but no constable was to be found; the people all wondering at me, as if I had been some strange Beast, or Monster brought out of Africa'. He appears, however, to have been enough of an eccentric himself to take the Mevagissey xenophobia in his stride. Despite his reception, he obviously stayed a while, and found time to describe the pilchard fishery: 'I was certified, that in that little town of Mevagissey there are 44 fisher boats, which do fish for pilchards, that every two boats have one net between them: they do call the two boats a seine, so there are 22 seines, and 22 nets . . .' He rambles on for some time in a similar vein, quoting a bewildering number of statistics, before concluding in masterly fashion: 'And now I hope I have filled my readers' bellies with pilchards, without cloying or offending their stomachs; if any one be queasy, or do feel a wambling in the gizzard; let them call for a cup of sack, drink it, and pay for it'. Exactly.

## THE TOWN AND HARBOUR

Taylor mentioned two taverns and six ale-houses in his day, and by the time of the new pier and harbour in the 1770s there were ten inns to serve the growing band of fishermen. As Frank Baron put it, in another poem from his wonderful collection *Mevagissey Backalong*:

> Low tide would leave the harbour dry,
> Flood tide surged up 'back revver',
> If mill-pool dropped, the mill-wheel stopped,
> But the beer flowed constant ever.

The beer still flows pretty constant in Mevagissey, and a few of the ten Georgian pubs survive, including the Ship where that first meeting of the harbour trustees took place and which dates back to the 17th century. According to Frank Baron it is the Fountain which has the greatest claim to be Mevagissey's oldest pub: 'The Fountain by Shill-alley-opp was father of them all'.

During the last war Mevagissey was defended against a German invasion by a Home Guard detachment stationed in the Harbour Master's office by the Watch House. They had nine rifles between them and a machine gun housed in the old lifeboat house. In the newly built up part of the quay wall by the Watch House you can see the nine holes for the rifles to poke through. There also used to be a chain drawn across the harbour mouth every night and taken up every morning, which was the sole responsibility of two retired naval men.

The lifeboat house which held the machine gun is now an aquarium; in 1930 Fowey gained a motor lifeboat and Mevagissey, being an intermediate station, was closed down. Originally the lifeboat had lived around the corner at Portmellon and was launched from the beach. Anyone who knows Portmellon in a gale will understand the difficulty: often the lifeboat crew were in more danger during launching than the crews they were intending to save. In 1897 the concrete boathouse and slipway were built in Mevagissey harbour; the building often sustained storm damage, but at least the boat could generally get a rapid launch.

On the opposite side of the harbour, Mevagissey's popular little museum occupies the old workshop and yard, built in 1745, of the town's first firm of boatbuilders. In later years it was Portmellon that became renowned for its boatbuilding, under the famous Percy Mitchell whose tale is told in *A Boat Builder's Story*.

## PORTMELLON AND CHAPEL POINT

To distract the eye from the systematic desecration going on inland from Portmellon, it is best to visit the cove in an easterly storm when it is a very exciting place indeed and the salt spray hides the new developments. The waves crash right over the road and hurl themselves against the blue-shuttered houses. The road was built just after the First World War; before then, coaches and cars and wagons had to be pushed across the beach.

From Portmellon, the coastal path leads out onto Chapel Point. Supposedly the site of the Bodrugan family's private chapel, this low, green point now supports the three sparkling white houses by J.A. Campbell which were built between 1934 and 1939 in a striking, but not at all jarring, style. Just beyond Turbot Point (the one beyond Chapel Point) is the place still called Bodrugan's Leap after Sir Henry's escape from Tudor justice.

## Pentewan

It is not far by road to Pentewan from Mevagissey, and a good walk along the coastal path past Polstreath, Penare Point and the ruined fishing settlement at Portgiskey; there is no choice but to go by land for it has been half a century since any boat has called at Pentewan harbour.

Visitors sometimes miss the village itself, believing the spread of caravans on the beach to be Pentewan, but the old settlement is tucked away to the north of the sands, around the edge of the dipping hills. Pentewan is a sad place; there is something tragic about its landlocked dock basin bearded with reeds, ducks dappling the water, the cottages grouped about with windows watching the empty harbour. There is an air of expectancy, of waiting—the old dock gates seem poised to open, the capstans ready to turn, and the rusty chains lying on the grassy wharfs like snakes in the sun seem to have only recently been laid down. The dock is stranded, separated from the sea by 400 yards of land: a channel choked with willows and reeds and then the high-banked sand of Pentewan beach.

## BUILDING THE HARBOUR

In 1818 work began, under the direction of local landlord, mining adventurer and MP Sir Christopher Hawkins, on a new harbour at Pentewan. Hawkins could see that another harbour was needed besides Charlestown, which was frequently congested, and he also wanted a private outlet for his own china clay pits: Pentewan was the natural choice. It had probably been an important harbour for many hundreds of years; it was the terminus of a prehistoric cross-county route over St Breock Downs, the Goss Moor and Hensbarrow Down, and it seems to have been more important than Mevagissey in the 13th and early 14th centuries. Stone from the quarry at Polrudden ('the beste free stone that Cornwall yealdeth', according to Norden in 1584) had been shipped from here

89

throughout the Middle Ages for the building of churches, and later Par harbour; and Leland had described Pentewan as a place 'witherto fischar Bootes repair for a Socour'.

Pentewan was still harbouring a small number of fishing boats at the beginning of the last century; a basin had been built to accommodate them, with cellars for curing and storing the fish, but it was not long before it fell into decay. Even before the new harbour was built, it was ill-starred; as early as 1739, Tonkin summed up what was to be Pentewan's one insuperable problem when he remarked that it 'would form a pretty little port were it not for the bar of sand made by waste brought down from the tin works, so that small craft only can get in, and that at spring tides'.

This silting had long since clogged up what used to be an estuary up as far as Nansladron Farm on the way to St Austell, and it was on the increase—ironically, because of the powdered quartz and mica waste pouring into the river from the clay works upstream. Thus it was the very industry which Pentewan was built to serve that condemned the port from the beginning.

The new harbour was built on the site of the old one, and the work involved deepening the existing basin and entrance channel, building quays and dock gates, protecting the entrance with a pier, installing cranes, and excavating a reservoir to help fill the basin and flush out the entrance. For the second purpose the reservoir, which was situated in the spur valley behind the post office and was only one-third of an acre in extent, was hopelessly inadequate. The port's misfortunes were not restricted to sand and silt: from the beginning progress was soured by overspending, a discontented workforce and shoddy workmanship.

By 1826 when work was completed, ships were already calling with coal for nearby mines and leaving loaded with china clay. A stone in the old part of the breakwater, now surrounded by sand, proudly bears the Hawkins arms, the date of completion and 'Sir C. H. BRT'. The success of the venture seemed ensured when, in 1829, a railway was built down the valley from St Austell (its route alongside the river can still be traced in places), but the line had one big drawback in that it was never extended backwards to reach the china clay works it was meant to serve. Nevertheless, it worked well for many years, avoiding the long journey for heavy wagons down the rough valley road.

## THE DECLINE OF PENTEWAN

Although there were years when Pentewan rivalled Charlestown, it was never popular with either clay owners or ship owners and captains. In February 1862 16 ships were detained in the port for five weeks because of sand in the channel, and sand blocking the river regularly caused floods to wash away sections of the railway.

In 1870 a string of four new reservoirs, with a combined water area of six acres, was dug along the floor of the main valley (the overgrown basin of the first one can be seen just before the little hump-backed bridge over the river) and there was from then on a much greater power to scour the

'. . . the landlocked dock basin, bearded with reeds . . .'

channel. Soon afterwards, however, came a fresh series of misfortunes—the china clay strike in 1913, competition from Par, the well-publicised detention of a steamer in the dock in 1914, and the closure of the railway in 1918—which slashed Pentewan's trade. The last load of clay was shipped in 1929, and the last trading ship called in 1940. For another twenty years or so it was still possible for a rowing boat to enter the harbour, but now the channel is dry land at even the highest tide.

The crowning irony is that now that the clay industry no longer dumps its waste in the river, Pentewan Beach is in danger of being eroded away.

## Charlestown

This privately owned working port, with an uncertain future, is the most fascinating harbour in Cornwall. It is also very beautiful, though travellers who came here when it was thriving considered it to be merely 'curious' or 'unlovely' or even, in one case, 'a gruesome pit'. They had not experienced the horrors of 20th century 'progress' and its effect on Cornwall's antique harbours, so they could not appreciate this undeveloped place with its extraordinary harmony of form. Charlestown is a Georgian Milton Keynes; a village planned and almost entirely built within two decades, and thus uncannily capturing the atmosphere of an age in its streets and houses.

## RASHLEIGH'S HARBOUR

In 1790 there was just a rocky little cove here called West Polmear or Porthmeor, with nine people, probably fishermen, living in the area. In 1801 the population had gone up to 281, and by 1851 there were nearly 3000 people living in the harbour village which was now called Charlestown to honour its creator, Charles Rashleigh. Like Hawkins, he was a local squire and mining adventurer; and the first to appreciate the need for a safe seaport for the rapidly expanding mining district around St Austell. By the late 18th century china clay was already being shipped from the exposed beach at West Polmear, and in 1791 Rashleigh began to build his harbour to the plans of John Smeaton, who designed the Eddystone Lighthouse and the new harbour at St Ives. A pier was begun in that year, largely for the security of fishing boats, and then, after it had been enlarged, the dock basin was started. It was a mammoth task—half the hillside had to be cut away and thousands of tons of solid rock removed—and still the problem of a water supply to the basin had to be overcome. For this vital supply, Rashleigh eventually went several miles inland to the head of the rocky and mysterious Luxulyan Valley, to the rushing Par River from which he built a watercourse, partly underground, all the way back to fill the two feeding reservoirs at Charlestown. He then, with considerable enterprise, built a series of watermills along both banks of the leat and let out the milling rights at £200 a year, in order to recoup some of his substantial losses.

Rashleigh then went on to establish a variety of harbourside industries: shipbuilding (which only ceased here within the last ten years), lime burning, brickmaking, net houses and bark houses, ropemaking (the old rope walk is still easy to spot, running straight up the hill to the right of the church between two lines of trees) and pilchard curing. Other businesses were attracted to the booming little port, like the highly successful foundry which was set up in 1827, and the still thriving pub called inevitably the Rashleigh Arms; and a protective battery was constructed up on the cliff southwest of the harbour, housing four 18-pounder guns during the French Wars.

At first the principal export was copper ore from local mines, but this was soon surpassed by china clay as the industry began to take off. Between 1850 and 1900 the clay industry doubled its output twice, while copper mining disappeared completely from the area. During the time when they were both booming and the port was also importing coal, timber, iron and limestone, the little dock often suffered from serious overcrowding and Par and Pentewan profited from Charlestown's growing reputation for delays and dangerous congestion.

## CHARLESTOWN TODAY

Even on the quietest of days there is the light dusting of china clay on the coloured cottages above the basin and on the dock walls and loading chutes to serve as a reminder that this is no open-air museum but a working port, in case you missed the proud blue signs which everywhere proclaim the same. There is every reason for pride when a small port is still trading, and it is the origin of Charlestown's special atmosphere.

There is nothing like the volume of traffic that there used to be, of course—Par and Fowey have the bulk of the china clay trade and, like all other ports, Charlestown's old diversity of imports has shrunk almost to nothing—but still the occasional coaster calls. In 1984, 94 ships came into Charlestown; 43,257 tonnes of clay and 3000 tonnes of grain were shipped out and 16,298 tonnes of fertilizer landed. The figures and cargoes vary from year to year depending on European economics and other inscrutable factors, and perhaps one day soon all the small ships will be scrapped and Charlestown will go into enforced but dignified retirement. Until then, this is a very exciting place to be when the bright and battered coasters call and the harbour bursts into life with lorries, cranes, engines chugging, little knots of people watching, and dockers brought up from Falmouth to help load and unload the ships. The best time of all to be here is when one of the coasters is arriving or leaving. It is the most dramatic and skilful operation to watch because the dock entrance, although widened in 1971 and provided with a new gate (which leans gracefully backwards before disappearing beneath the water to lie on the bottom), is still painfully narrow. A ship of 500 tons has only nine inches to spare on either side and nine inches under her keel when loaded. There is also a sharp turn in the outer harbour, to line up with the entrance, where the almost inevitable swell makes it that much more difficult to be accurate. God forbid that Charlestown should ever lose its struggle for survival and become just another has-been port selling plastic imitations of its memories.

Up above the dock, behind the new (and highly thought of) shipwreck centre, is the disused china clay 'dry' with its overgrown settling tanks behind. From the dry, a tunnel which used to carry an underground tramway runs down to the dock wall; there the clay-filled trucks would come out in a gallery in the wall from which chutes fed the clay into the ships' holds below. Now the clay is dried elsewhere, and lorries deliver it into chutes fixed at road level above the old galleries. The china clay dry is an exception; for a port with a busy past, Charlestown has remarkably few empty buildings and there are enough small but thriving businesses, such as the Cornish Smoked Fish Company, tucked away in old lofts and warehouses to dispel the threatening air of dilapidation. For the most haunting evocation of Charlestown, seek out A. L. Rowse's poem 'Charlestown Harbour' from his 'Poems Chiefly Cornish'.

## Par

Sadly, the harbour that dominates St Austell Bay with its huge china clay dries and chimneys in a fine haze of clay dust, which is one of the most interesting in Cornwall, is private and entirely commercial and thus, by rights, has no place in this book. But a small place must be found for Par, so that mention can be made of the remarkable Joseph Thomas Treffry.

*'. . . a bustle of ships . . .'*

The story of the three planned ports of Pentewan, Charlestown and Par is the story of three great Cornish entrepreneurs, and the greatest of them was J. T. Treffry. Not only did he build Par harbour in a most unpromising and hazardous situation, establish an industrial hot-house in the wild Luxulyan Valley, and link the two with one of his canals, but he was also involved in a staggering number of schemes and businesses throughout mid-Cornwall which included copper mining, granite quarrying, shipping, china clay, and the building of roads and railways.

The transformation of the Par area had begun some time before J. T. Treffry started to build his harbour; only 200 years ago the area now covered by the Par docks, the town of Par and the new parts of St Blazey was under the sea. This was a broad tidal estuary, the shape of which can be seen from the contour lines on an Ordnance Survey map, and its disappearance is an extraordinary example of the power of river-borne silt and mining waste. Cornish place names in the area testify to the extent of the estuary: Tywardreath is 'the house on the sand', and a finger of the sea once crept up to touch the walls of the medieval priory there; the old name of St Blazey, Landreath, means 'the church on the sand'; and Treesmill, further inland still at the head of a strange marshy valley, has nothing to do with trees at all, but comes from the same Cornish roots as Millendreath, up near Looe, meaning 'the mill on the sand'.

At high tide there used to be a ferry across the estuary for travellers on the ancient coast road through Cornwall, running from just below Tywardreath to a point near the Par Inn, and at low tide it seems that the passage could be forded, with care. A plaque on the wall of the bakery, just up from the Par Inn, bears the words 'On this site stood the Sloop Inn. Nearby a sloop foundered c. 1777'. Although by then the ferry was no longer running, the tide still reached St Blazey Church.

## TREFFRY'S HARBOUR

When J. T. Treffry came, in the 1820s, to look for an outlet for his rich copper mines at Lanescot that was nearer and easier to get to than Fowey, he decided to build an artificial harbour at the far end of a sandbank (now Par Beach) which was building up across the estuary mouth, and upon which small vessels had already begun to load and discharge cargoes. He at first used the celebrated engineer James Meadows Rendel (who also drew up the plans for the harbour at Loe Pool) to plan the harbour, but then sacked him in an atmosphere of acrimony and went ahead with his own designs for a breakwater to be built along the line of a reef called Spit Rocks. A hundred and fifty years later, by a sweet irony, much of the expansion and improvement to the harbour was carried out by the descendents of the same unlucky J. M. Rendel. Treffry's 1,200 foot breakwater enclosed 36 acres of harbour, much of which was filled in and built up with rubble and granite, and within a few years it was capable of accommodating 50 vessels of up to 200 tons.

J. T. Treffry would recognize very little of his harbour if he was to return today; the long central pier and the breakwater are in their original positions, despite much expansion, but of the many industries he established on the site—a smelting works (with a famous 237 foot stack, felled in 1907), a brickworks (the row of sheds along the edge of the docks, in Harbour Road, are made of Par bricks), a pilchard fishery, shipbuilding yards, sail lofts, granite cutting and dressing yards, a candle-making factory, a chandlery, limekilns, blacksmiths' and carpenters' shops, a flour mill—barely a trace remains. The only original building left is the old blacksmiths' shop which is now the rigging shed and can be seen straight ahead through the dock gates. Since Par was bought from the Treffrys in the late 1940s its trade, like its on-site businesses, has been concerned with just one commodity, china clay.

There is often a bustle of ships in St Austell Bay waiting to go into the harbour on the tide, and with the new design of coasters (some are more like barges, with a shallow draft and all their superstructure aft), Par can take ships of up to 2300 tons and can berth eleven at a time. Since the 1960s Fowey has become the main china clay port because it can take much larger vessels than Par at all stages of the tide. Although Par handled 646 ships in 1984 to Fowey's 604, they carried less than half the amount of clay carried from Fowey. Despite its handicaps and its tricky entrance, Par remains one of the busiest and most important of Cornwall's harbours, and a fitting tribute to the vision of its creator.

## Polkerris

On the far side of St Austell Bay, the old harbour and hamlet of Polkerris, Betjeman's 'little half-moon shuttered cove', huddles in a wooded cleft of the Gribben. Charlestown may be the most conspicuous illustration of Rashleigh patronage, but this is the very heart of Rashleigh country. Charlestown stemmed from one energetic individual; here we are looking at the slow shaping of centuries of Rashleigh influence. It is almost imperceptible, but there is something feudal about Polkerris; it still has the air of a private manorial fishing cove. The village is remarkably undeveloped—a sure sign that a powerful family lurks nearby—and yet it has escaped the awful taint of preciousness; it is Cornish enough to have a healthy scattering of corrugated iron, skeletal boats and derelict sheds saving it from being just too pretty.

On still summer evenings the low sun gets caught here, embayed in the cove, reflecting off the old stone walls and cottage windows, and people come by boat, by car and on foot to sit on the pub terrace and watch the sun go down over St Austell Bay.

### THE PILCHARD FISHERY

St Austell Bay we call it now, but it was once known as Polkerris Bay, in honour of the most important fishing station along this stretch of coast. It is only right that Polkerris today should still be dominated by the ruins of its pilchard cellars, slumbering magnificently on the beach. No wonder cellars were often known as palaces or castles; these particular ones, which claim to be the largest in the county, have the look of a great medieval fort built to defend the tiny harbour.

You can get a good view of the layout of the cellars by climbing up behind them; from where you can see down into the roofless building. Across both ends are the large apartments used to house coal and salt. You can still make out the wide entrance tunnels running through them. On the landward side, the courtyard wall adjoins the cliff and supports one side of a simple ridge roof, the inner edge of which rests on pillars. Under this roof the fish were bulked. The opposite side is similar but has an upper storey in which the fishermen slept during the season and stored their gear.

It is clear that Polkerris was an important fishing cove for hundreds of years; Norden, for instance, writing in 1584, describes it as a place 'wher

*Polkerris—'. . . the low sun gets caught here, embayed in the cove . . .'*

great store of Pilchardes are taken at the time of the yeare', and in his map of West Hundred, several boats are depicted shooting seine nets off Polkerris with 'pilchard fishinge' written alongside. The curving slate pier was built in the 1730s for the protection of the fishing fleet by Jonathon Rashleigh. The cellars, also a Rashleigh foundation, might well be older; there is mention of 'a seine house' at Polkerris in 1590. By the late 19th century the pilchards had almost ceased to visit this part of the coast, and the fisheries all along the South Coast had dwindled away; in the 1870s there was only one seine and two drift nets, with their boats, left at Polkerris. The old lifeboat house, in use until the boat was removed to Fowey in 1922, is now a café, across the slipway from the pub. The present pub building used to be a boatshed; the old pub was next door in what is now the car park and was swept away by the sea one stormy night.

## RASHLEIGH COUNTRY

The coastal path to the Gribben first zig-zags up the nearly perpendicular valley side with its light dusting of woodland, before striding out in the open above the tiny beaches and coves which pucker the low cliffs. At Gribben Head, beckoning you onwards and looking good enough to eat, is the 84 foot tall red and white landmark which was built in 1832:

> Fragile and rosy in evening light,
> Behind, the lovely headland lies,
> The landmark loved of mariners
> Catches the last glow in the skies.

(A. L. Rowse, from 'The Gribben: Palm Sunday, 1943')

97

You can return to Polkerris by way of Polridmouth (pronounced Prid-mouth) Beach and Menabilly Barton, then along the lane past Trega-minion Church. This is as close as you will get to Menabilly itself, the Rashleigh family's ancestral seat, which was for many years the beloved home of Daphne du Maurier and was the 'Manderley' of her famous novel *Rebecca*. Like the Rashleigh influence, you can never quite see Menabilly (except as a glimpse in the distance from up near the Gribben) but you know it is there.

The lonely little church of Tregaminion, a surprising thing to find in a copse in the midst of farmland, is of Rashleigh foundation, a votive offering from William Rashleigh upon his succession to the family estate. Its role turned out to be more tragic than celebratory for the family: of William's daughters commemorated within, we are told that Rachel died aged four, Charlotte aged two, Harriet aged nine, Caroline-Mary aged eight and Jane aged thirty.

On the hill above Polkerris, at the head of the valley, is Kilmarth which has been the home of Daphne du Maurier since she left Menabilly and was the setting for her extraordinary novel *The House on the Strand*. Devotees of this book, which describes with such uncanny clarity the old estuarine landscape here, can easily retrace the steps of Dick Young from Kilmarth to Tywardreath, and beyond to the Treesmill Valley, a beautiful but chilling place—'the strange sweep of the valley, no pattern of fields, nothing but a tapestry of willow, birch and alder'—which, in the 14th century 'lay submerged beneath a sheet of water, part of a great winding estuary that cut into the land'.

*Fowey*—'"... *flights of stone steps, overhung by great pink tufts of valerian*

# 6  The Fowey Estuary

O the Harbour of Fowey
Is a beautiful spot,
And it's there I enjowey
To sail in a yot;
Or to race in a yacht
Round a mark or a buoy—
Such a beautiful spacht
Is the Harbour of Fuoy!

When her anchor is weighed
And the water she ploughs,
Upon neat lemoneighed
O it's then I caroughs;
And I take Watt's hymns
And I sing them aloud
When it's homeward she skymns
O'er the waters she ploud.

But the wave mountain-high,
And the violent storm,
Do I risk them? Not Igh!
But prefer to sit worm
With a book on my knees
By the library fire,
While I list to the brees
Rising hire and hire.

And so, whether I weigh
Up the anchor or not,
I am happy each deigh
In my home or my yot;
Every care I resign,
Every comfort enjoy,
In this cottage of mign
By the Harbour of Foy.

Q, 'The Harbour of Fowey' from *A Fowey Garland*

THROUGHOUT history, sailors have sought desperately for a glimpse of the narrow embrace of Fowey Harbour. They tended to miss this rocky entrance, often with tragic consequences, and over the years a variety of structures have been pressed into service as seamarks.

In the Middle Ages a bell and a light were hung in the window of St Catherine's Chapel, on the Fowey side of the harbour mouth. After the chapel fell into disuse (there is no trace left of it now), the old windmill up at the top of the town, of which only the stump remains, was used; and then the church tower at Lanlivery, despite being six miles inland and partially screened by hills, served for a time and was whitewashed with the aid of a grant from the Fowey Corporation. Perhaps the most enduring seamark has been St Saviour's Chapel, high on the hill above Polruan. All that remains of it now is one massive corner, an ancient stone finger reaching upwards, from a rash of modern buildings, towards the sky. It occupies a similar position to the chapel of the same name which stood above Padstow harbour, and doubtless both were built to guide lost souls in the physical sense as much as the spiritual.

Since the last century, Fowey has been much easier to find from afar thanks to the tower built as a day mark by Trinity House for that very purpose on Gribben Head, and to the flashing light near St Catherine's Point.

## Fowey

In the 14th century (we are told by Leland, writing 200 years on) Fowey was 'hauntid with Shippes of diverse Nations, and their Shippes went to al Nations', and six centuries later this is still the essence of the place. Some aspects have changed; there is nothing like the variety of trade which once passed through Fowey, and the port can no longer be regarded as one of the foremost in Britain, as it was in the Middle Ages. We are told by a later source that in 1346 Fowey contributed 47 ships and 770 men to the siege of Calais. This is quite possibly an exaggeration, but what matters is that it was the largest recorded contribution of any English port, and the chronicler obviously did not see it as unlikely that this should be so.

### THE TOWN

Fowey has long been dominated by the great mansion of Place, an ancient house with more recent additions, including the gloriously eccentric tower of Porphry Hall, unmistakably the work of J. T. Treffry. Home of the Treffry family for over 500 years, it stands aloof and protected from the old mercantile section of the town which huddles along the river from Town Quay up to Caffa Mill Pill. Bridging the gulf between the two is the church of St Fimbarrus, with its fine tower of Polrudden stone which is said to be the second tallest in Cornwall, after Probus. Inside the church there is a mass of Treffry memorials, including a window dedicated to the great J. T. Treffry, and a brass of Elizabeth Treffry, defender of Fowey against the French, and an unassuming little brass plaque in one of the pews which simply states that it is 'In loving memory of Sir Arthur and Lady Quiller-Couch who frequently worshipped in this pew'. There is also a wonderful seascape window in the tower, accompanied by the moving verse 'Ho, everyone that thirsteth, come ye to the waters . . .'.

Parts of the Town Hall are 15th century, and other noteworthy buildings include the Ship Inn (once a Rashleigh town house), the Lugger Inn, 'Noah's Ark' in Fore Street, and 9 South Street (the Treffry Estate Office). It is always worth lifting your eyes above the shops which so unconsciously occupy the old houses or, better still, walking up along Bull Hill, above Fore Street, from where you can look down on the secluded jumble of their telltale roofs and walls and yards. Much of the river side of Fore Street and North Street, now packed with houses, was once taken up with the many private merchants' wharves; remnants of those days are the Harbour Commissioners' Wharf, where the Fowey Gallants now have their dinghy park, and Berrill's Wharf, now a private car park further along North Street where coal was still landed until about 30 years ago.

## To Readymoney Cove and the Gribben

The southern limit of old Fowey used to be marked by the South Gate, an arched gatehouse built over the narrow end of Lostwithiel Street, between the Ship Inn and the Toll Bar. A similar structure also spanned the road just beyond the Riverside Hotel at the town's northern end.

Walking uphill from the site of the South Gate and along the Esplanade towards Readymoney Cove, takes you through the newer, richer Fowey where the houses have room to breathe and the pedestrian is given frequent uninterrupted views of the harbour. Just beyond Whitehouse slip, whence for centuries the passenger ferry has plied to Polruan, is The Haven, beloved home for much of his life of Sir Arthur Quiller-Couch, the great novelist and scholar who wrote under the pen-name of 'Q' and whose love for Fowey, the 'Troy Town' of his writings, made the town famous the world over. Many people love Fowey, but few have the gift to write of that love as effortlessly as Q when, in *Memories and Opinions*, he describes his first visit here:

'That night before undressing I stood long and gazed on the harbour, the track of the moon on its water, the riding lights of two or three small schooners at anchor in the shadow of the farther shore, and decided that this were no bad place in which to live. And that is all I need say here of my first acquaintance with the upper and lower reaches of an estuary the tides of which time has since woven so close into the pulse of my own life that memory cannot now separate the rhythms.'

Further along, in a magnificent position overlooking Readymoney Cove on the site of an 18th century three-gun battery, stands Point Neptune House. Now divided into flats, it was built in the last century by William Rashleigh who preferred it to his ancestral seat at Menabilly. St Catherine's Parade, a beautiful walkway under a vault of trees, was the entrance drive to the house and later given over to the people of Fowey for their recreation. High up on top of the far hill above Readymoney is the extraordinary Rashleigh Mausoleum, a huge crown of stone over the resting-place of William, his wife and his daughter, built on the probable site of the old chapel of St Catherine's.

101

Readymoney, a misty knot of cottages in winter, is often too crowded in summer to be appreciated; that little patch of sand is highly prized in Fowey where beaches are scarce. The way up to St Catherine's Castle from here is, for the first part, along an ancient green lane, the bare rock of its surface carrying the wheel-scores of generations of carts which trundled down to Readymoney to collect sand, seaweed or burnt lime to dress the acid soils of the local farms. The old limekilns have been almost unrecognizably converted into a turreted sitting area down in the cove.

St Catherine's Castle perches on the cliff edge like a toy fort, perfect in proportion for children to play in but too small, surely, for fully-grown soldiers. It was built in about 1540 by Thomas Treffry, who also built St Mawes Castle, as part of Henry VIII's chain of defences along the Channel coast, and the later gun platform cut into the cliff below was last used in the Second World War. There is a tiny grassy place, a very special corner, high up around the far side of the castle above a precipitous drop, where you can sit for hours in the warm angle of the old walls and look out on nothing but sea.

From the castle, a walk along the coast path of about two miles will lead you to the Gribben via the tiny, perfect Coombe Valley and the two beaches at Polridmouth. Was it while walking along this stretch of coastline and back again to Fowey that Kenneth Grahame was inspired to create that wonderful part of *The Wind in the Willows* which is called 'Wayfarers All'? Friends of his later suggested that this was so. Grahame was a great friend of Q's and a frequent visitor to The Haven, he was even married in Fowey's St Fimbarrus Church, and in 'Wayfarers All' the Sea Rat gives the Water Rat, and us, a description of Fowey which is perhaps the most memorable of all:

'"And now," he was softly saying, "I take to the road again, holding on southwestwards for many a long and dusty day; till at last I reach the little grey sea town I know so well, that clings along one steep side of the harbour. There through dark doorways you look down flights of stone steps, overhung by great pink tufts of valerian and ending in a patch of sparkling blue water. The little boats that lie tethered to the rings and stanchions of the old sea-wall are as gaily painted as those I clambered in and out of in my own childhood; the salmon leap on the flood tide, schools of mackerel flash and play past quay-sides and foreshores, and by the windows the great vessels glide, night and day, up to their moorings or forth to the open sea."'

## Polruan

Polruan has suffered from becoming, for many people, no more than the view from Fowey, and despite some criminal skyline development (perhaps the most crazy piece of planning in the whole of Cornwall), the charm of that view remains. There is much more to Polruan than meets the Fowey-based eye, however. There is a strange remoteness and isolation here, quite different from the cosmopolitan atmosphere across the water, and Fowey people have long referred to Polruan as 'Little Russia'.

It seems likely that Polruan has had a longer history than its more famous neighbour. The great Cornish historian Charles Henderson wrote, earlier this century: 'I am of the opinion that a visitor to Fowey in the year 1066 would have found but a Celtic church and few fishermen's houses . . . and that Polruan would have been the main centre of trade and population at the estuary mouth'. Subsequently, Polruan languished without the backing of a powerful feudal patron and Fowey soon over-shadowed it in size and importance. Polruan's ties with the sea were always strong—she too provided ships for the King's service, harboured pirates, and engaged in overseas trade—but the inevitable comparisons with Fowey tended to belittle the town's position and achievements. The two really should not be compared at all because they have developed quite separately and at their own pace over the centuries. Despite the ancient ferry crossings, the Fowey River has always been a dividing line. Polruan has always had more in common with the remote landscape of scattered farms and plunging lanes behind it than with the town it faces across the harbour.

In the last century there was something of a renaissance in Polruan's centuries-old boatbuilding industry, encouraged by the demand of the infant china clay trade for locally built schooners. Fowey also built many ships then, but at Polruan there is a rare sense of continuity and that busy time is not just another memory, for at Toms Yard by the quay there is still a flourishing business on the site of the famous Slades Yard which turned out so many fine ships in the 19th century. The Slade family and their boatyard formed the basis of Daphne du Maurier's novel *The Loving Spirit*, and Toms Yard now is not so very different from Slades Yard then (Coombes in the book) with 'the great trunks of trees, old and well seasoned, that lay waiting to be cut for planks, the sawdust on the ground, the smell of new rope and tar and the rough unformed shapes of boats'.

From Polruan's main street, which climbs boldly straight up the hill, a narrow lane runs past the Russell Inn and on to the old castle, a ruined blockhouse squatting firmly on the rocks at the harbour mouth. Over on the Fowey side you can just make out the remains of a twin blockhouse which has suffered more severely from storm and decay. There is some disagreement as to whether these great defensive structures were built in the late 13th or late 14th century. They were definitely meant to protect Fowey harbour from foreign attack, but whether as a result of the Spanish raid in 1380 or the French one in 1457, historians cannot decide. During the latter attack much of Fowey was burned and the French were only finally repulsed by the efforts of Elizabeth Treffry, a splendid woman who, besieged in Place with little ammunition left, stripped the lead off the roof of her great house, melted it down and poured it over the Frenchmen below. Between the two blockhouses there used to hang a huge chain to defend Fowey from her many enemies, but later this was probably forcibly removed as the piracy and general lawlessness of the Fowey sailors became an unacceptable embarrassment to an English monarchy striving for peace on the high seas.

## THE HALL WALK

Although it is a delight to cross the harbour from Fowey in the small passenger ferry, many people prefer to approach Polruan by a much longer route, the well known and loved Hall Walk. It begins in Bodinnick, across the water from Caffa Mill where there used to be an inlet that was the centre of much of Fowey's boatbuilding industry. The car ferry from Caffa Mill to Bodinnick used to depart from the steep slip by the Riverside Hotel until a few years ago, and there has been a ferry crossing here for over six centuries, and probably considerably longer for this is where the ancient coast road, one of the three major routes through Cornwall, crossed the Fowey. It has long since ceased to be a great artery of communication, but things might have been very different, and the development of Bodinnick and Fowey dramatically altered, had Joseph Thomas Treffry had his way in the last century. It was the desire of that great Cornish entrepreneur to build a grand suspension bridge across the Fowey at this point (with 120 foot towers at each end and the roadway 98 feet above the water), as part of a larger scheme to provide an improved coast road from Torpoint to St Austell. But for a last-minute lack of support it might so easily have gone ahead; as it is, it was one of the very few plans of J. T. Treffry that came to nothing.

In crossing the river on the ferry, the eye is inevitably caught by a building all alone on the water's edge 250 yards downstream from Bodinnick which many people consider to be the most charming place on the river. This is Prime Cellars, a corruption of 'Priam's Cellars', and it was once an ale-house serving the floating population of Fowey harbour, as did the White House at Falmouth. Up behind it climbs an old garden which was owned and loved by Q for many years; 'Little Tonkin's Garden', he called it, or sometimes 'The Farm' or 'The Wilderness'. This is how he describes the garden in *News from the Duchy*, as a preface to relating its history: 'From the cliff overhanging the rear of the cellars a wilderness climbs the hillside, terrace by terrace; based with a line of sizeable trees that droop their boughs to the high tides, and mounting through orchards of apple, pear, plum, cherry, and thickets of hawthorn, blackthorn, spindlewood, elder, to a high amphitheatre which is all gorse and bracken, with here and there a holly or an ilex standing up from the undergrowth. The fruit trees are decrepit, twisted with age or by the climbing ivy. The cherries have reverted to savagery, and serve only to make a pretty show of blossom in April. No one knows when they were planted for human delight: but planted they once were, and for that purpose, for my wilderness six hundred years ago for certain—and possibly seven or eight hundred years ago—was a terraced garden, pleasance of the great house that stood where now stands the farmstead of Hall, a little beyond the brow of the hill.'

Right alongside the ferry slip is the enchanting 'Ferryside', once a boatbuilder's yard and sail loft, which has belonged to the du Maurier family since the 1920s. On the corner of the house is mounted the figurehead of the *Jane Slade*, the schooner built at Slades Yard in Polruan which gave Daphne du Maurier her first inspiration for *The Loving Spirit* in which Jane Slade and her namesake ship are renamed Janet Coombe. In *Vanishing Cornwall*, Daphne du Maurier describes her first sight of Fowey harbour, from the garden of this 'strange looking house, built like a Swiss chalet', with the same eloquence as did Q in his *Memories and Opinions*: 'I went and stood beneath the chalet, the water immediately beneath me, and looked towards the harbour mouth. There were small boats everywhere, and yachts at anchor, but more stirring still a big ship was drawing near, with two attendant tugs, to moor a few cables' length from the house itself. There was a smell in the air of tar and rope and rusted chain, a smell of tidal water. Down harbour, around the point, was the open sea. Here was the freedom I desired, long sought-for, not yet known.'

Bodinnick, spared the effects of a major trunk route, still struggles gamely up the steep hill beside the old road as it has done for centuries. One of the great attractions of the Hall Walk, for some, is that if you walk slowly enough you can leave the Old Ferry Inn in Bodinnick as 'Time' is being called at half past two, and arrive at the Russell or the Lugger in Polruan at opening time in the evening.

The walk begins partway up Bodinnick hill, on the right, and its first section, as far as Penleath Point where Q's memorial overlooks his adored harbour, is the Hall Walk proper. It was a private promenade created in the 16th century by the Mohun family of Hall, the most important manor in this area and now a farm. The Hall Walk narrowly avoided becoming a place of national importance during the Civil War when, in August 1644, King Charles I was just missed by someone taking a pot shot at him from Fowey, as he strolled along it. An extremely unlucky, nameless, fisherman was killed instead, and the king was able to live for another five years before being executed officially.

From Penleath Point the path turns and follows Pont Pill up to the head of the creek and back around to Polruan.

The Hall Walk makes Pont Pill an exception, but generally the Fowey estuary is best explored by boat, and in one of shallow draft (such as those on hire from Town Quay) you can reach Lostwithiel, as well as Lerryn and Penpoll, on a high spring tide.

## Up the River

*FOWEY DOCKS*

Beyond Caffa Mill the English China Clay jetties begin, and although many people have written with relief of their secluded position which keeps Fowey postcards blemish-free, to others this is the exciting part— the beating heart of a living, working river. On average, thirteen ships a week make their way upstream to the docks. They are usually small, brightly-coloured coasters barely given a second glance (they seem almost to scale), but when one of the great Leviathans of 16,000 or 17,000 tonnes (the *Astrea* or the *Pollux*) enters the harbour, most people pause to watch. Dwarfing the houses and wooded hills, she makes her stately progress up the crowded river, dinghies scurrying from her path; and if she comes at night, the waterside cottages gently shake as a massive bank of lights, like a floating city, glides slowly past their windows.

China clay has been shipped from Fowey for over 100 years, but in the last fifteen or so this narrow slither of docks sandwiched between the whitened wooded hillside and the river has seen something of a revolution. English China Clay's main port of Par could not cope with the larger ships of the 1960s, so the company acquired a 200 year lease on Fowey docks from British Rail in 1968, converted the old Par–Fowey railway into a private road and set about pumping capital into the decaying docks. After about £8 million had been spent on the jetties and the highly advanced system of conveyors which can move 1000 tonnes of clay an hour, ECC found that the hillside was slowly moving down upon their golden half-mile and so more money, and another two years, had to be spent pinning it back with steel rods and concrete.

It is not only the efficiency of the docks, which exported over 1·6 million tonnes of clay in 1986 in the form of dry powder and wet slurry, that has undergone a transformation, but also the relationship between the docks and the town. Gone are the days when the visiting crews would stock up on food and clothes in Fowey, and when several businesses existed almost entirely on their trade. Modern ships are in and out of the docks so quickly, and are so well-stocked, that the economy of the town has had to turn from the ships to the yachts to find a growing market. Never before have the docks been so divorced from Fowey as they are now, and the visiting ships made so little impact upon the life of the town.

The last jetty, No. Eight, marks the end of the Lostwithiel–Fowey railway which used to continue to the old station at Caffa Mill where the Fowey–Par line began. This glorious line, which runs for its entire length right alongside the river, was closed to passengers on January 4, 1965, but saved from a complete shutdown by the docks' need for clay which is now trundled down the line, past chestnut woods and families of swans, in long strings of rattling wooden trucks. The trains no longer pause at Golant Halt for shoppers, workers or schoolchildren going to Fowey or Lost-withiel: for Golant, the railway was a vital link and the village is now cut off from any form of public transport.

## GOLANT

Given its wonderful position, Golant is not as attractive as it should be, nor as it was when in the early part of this century it was a favourite place for people from Fowey to boat up to, for tea at the New Inn (now the Fisherman's Arms) or at Mrs Rundle's. L. Duncombe-Jewell described it in 1901: 'Golant, embowered in orchards of apple, pear and plum trees, presents in springtime a rare spectacle of pink and white blossom; while in the autumn the nights are vocal with the noise of falling fruit, whose juice is expressed amid the mud of its curious entanglement of lanes by the feet of the incautious pedestrian'. The orchards have mostly disappeared now under a jumble of modern housing. A few apple orchards remain, but of the six stone cider presses operating in the village within living memory only one, which used to belong to Reg Tabb whose cider was renowned for miles around, still exists.

The village still has some attractions, some real life left—there are still boat builders and engineers down by the water, and then there is the tiny Fore Street, heart of the old Golant, with the Fisherman's Arms at its lower end, and the beautiful church of St Sampson's nestling high above the river—well worth the steep climb up to it which must have been a severe test of the villagers' religious fervour over the centuries. This is an ancient holy place, although the present church is late-medieval, and the possible site of a small monastery or religious cell founded in the 6th century by St Sampson, the best known of all the Celtic saints who travelled between Ireland, Wales and Brittany.

There is a fine walk back to Fowey from Golant across the high common which falls away steeply in a riot of bracken and brambles to the river below. The path leads you past the old sawmills (now a sophisticated recording studio to which musicians and their instruments come by boat) on an inlet called Bodmin Pill. It is so called because it was from these old quays that Bodmin merchants, who were always active in maritime trade despite coming from an inland town, used to work. The way then leads up through the hush of the woods, on the same path used by the Bodmin merchants, to join the old road from Lostwithiel to Fowey near Penventinue.

## PENPOLL

Opposite Golant is Penpoll Creek, a quiet and lonely stretch of water idling between fields dotted with herons standing motionless like saplings on the hillside. A little way up, on the left, is the beautiful house of St Cadix, gazing across the river, on the site of a small monastery which dated back to before the Norman Conquest and continued until the Reformation.

At the head of the creek are the hamlets of Middle and Lower Penpoll with some fine old limekilns and a disused water mill which, according to L. Duncombe-Jewell, used to grind corn for Plymouth Docks and the Royal Navy in the days of Nelson, although it is hard to believe that they could not find somewhere nearer at hand.

## CLIFF

Back on the Fowey River, the next waterside settlement above Golant is at Cliff, on the other side. Like Golant, Cliff used to be a popular place for boating parties to stop for tea. However, Cliff is an ancient settlement which grew up not because of the fame of its tea-gardens but because of the

*Penpoll—'". . . some fine old limekilns . . ."'*

passage across the river here—a low-water ford with a submerged cause-way—which played an important strategic role in the Civil War. The diary of Richard Symonds, an officer in the King's army, records that on August 17, 1644 (shortly before the shooting incident on the Hall Walk) '. . . His Majestie . . . went to Cliffe, a parish on this side of the river that runs to Listithiel, where Colonel Lloyd the Quarter-Master Generall's regiment lyes to keepe the passe. The enemye keepes the passe on the other side at the parish of Glant.' The Parliamentarians, sandwiched in the peninsula between Fowey and Tywardreath, were eventually driven out of Cornwall, and the county then remained in Royalist hands until near the end of the war.

## LERRYN

Beyond Cliff the river forks, with the main Fowey River on the left and Lerryn Creek on the right. Lerryn is the most popular destination of all on the river these days. The creek is more enclosed than Penpoll; nestling between high wooded hills with the branches of trees caressing the water, it curls past the scarcely seen remains of many tiny quays which used to trade in timber, charcoal and oak bark, and flour from the mills hidden deep in the woods.

Ethy Rock, a grass-covered rocky outcrop jutting into the river, fringed with old quay walls, is a favourite and often over-popular picnic spot. To

*Lerryn bridge—'. . . a rough little medieval gem'*

get this creek to yourself you have to walk down from Lerryn (along the footpath through the trees) at low tide when a multitude of birds peppers the great expanse of shining mudbanks and the silence is broken only by their calls.

Up until the late 1960s there used to be a regatta at Lerryn every summer. It was a marvellous occasion when boats of all shapes and sizes would race up from Fowey and Golant on the tide, those with shallow draft gaining a head start on the larger, more powerful craft. The only rules were: four to a boat with no-one allowed to get out and push. What a spectacle greeted them as they rounded the final bend and came in sight of the village: people and fairground stalls thronged the right bank, there were swingboats and merry-go-rounds, toffee apples and dancing monkeys, a mud race at low tide, then the greasy pole and tossing the hay bale later. In the early evening, young families had picnic teas in the many boats moored all the way along the waterfront, while those who were old enough repaired for their refreshment to the Ship Inn.

Lerryn was quite an important trading place in its time, dealing mostly with agricultural produce (destined for Devonport market or for sale to ships in Fowey harbour) and materials such as coal, sand, seaweed and limestone. There are still two sets of limekilns in the village, one in a state of dignified decay, the other strangely incorporated into the foundations of a house. In the 19th century Lerryn also became the port for the Herodsfoot Gunpowder Mills, nine miles to the east, which provided explosives for Cornish mines. Local people can well remember the barges which used to ply up the river with their loads of saltpetre and sulphur, and back down again with gunpowder.

Like most of the tiny ports on Cornwall's main rivers, Lerryn's commercial river traffic began to peter out with the development of the railways and an improved road system. Duncombe-Jewell's age, when 'occasionally vessels of over a hundred tons burden still surprise the boating man as he comes out between the overhanging trees into the "harbour" of Lerryn' is now gone for good.

## *PENQUITE*

Above Cliff the main river goes up to Lostwithiel past the mansion of Penquite, high up on the left, now a youth hostel. It was here that Garibaldi came to stay in 1864. His host was Colonel Peard, whose efforts to help the Italian patriots had earned him the name of 'Garibaldi's Englishman'. When Garibaldi came to leave Penquite, he was rowed downriver to Albert Quay where a decorated arch had been erected, and inscribed with the words 'May health and blessing attend thee. Farewell Garibaldi.'

After Colonel Peard, a china clay magnate called Frank Parkyn lived at Penquite, and local rumour still has it that Edward VII used to visit him and indulge in Bacchanalian revels down in the little boathouse by the river. The 'pleasure-house' as it is more commonly known, is now a sad ruin—sad because it was obviously once such an elegant place—and the rumours have never been substantiated, but for a stone from the jetty wall (now at Penquite) which has the king's name carved upon it.

## *ST WINNOW*

A little way up from Penquite, on the opposite side of the river, is the tiny churchtown of St Winnow, considered by many to be the most beautiful spot on the Fowey. Not only is the setting of church, old farm buildings and vicarage almost perfect, but this serene place has had a long and interesting history.

St Winnow must have been an important trading place for many hundreds of years, and perhaps a religious establishment was first founded here (long before the Conquest) because it was a well-known landing place on one of the main navigable rivers of the Southwest. Throughout the Middle Ages the influence of the church was considerable (it was the mother church for a very large parish) and the quay gradually took on more trade as Lostwithiel declined as a port, including the important slate trade from the St Neot quarries. Leland wrote of St Winnow in the mid-16th century: 'By this Chirch is a Warfe to make Shippes by'; the old quay is still there, built a little way out from the shore beside the wide bend of the channel, but the ships have long since ceased to call.

## Lostwithiel

In the approach to Lostwithiel the valley broadens and the river narrows to a small channel which winds through the strange silent marshland of

Shirehall Moor and Madderly Moor. Ahead, a ring of higher land encloses the town of Lostwithiel, whose position is heralded by the huge square tower of a milk factory which seems to float in the distance above the scrubland. It may seem as though you are approaching a space-age city but Lostwithiel, dominated (before the tower was built) by the beautiful spire of St Bartholomew's Church and the castle of Restormel on a hill behind, is an old place with perhaps the most fascinating history of any Cornish town.

It is an unassuming town which makes little of its glorious past; it is hard to guess that it was once the administrative capital of the county, under the patronage of the Earls, and then the Dukes, of Cornwall, or that for a time it was the sole port for Cornish tin, its foreign trade greater in value than that of all the Cinque Ports put together, giving it second place on the South Coast to Southampton. There are still substantial remains of the 13th century Duchy buildings to be seen, and a fine strong 15th century bridge over the Fowey River, but there is scarcely a hint that it was once such a thriving port. The old quay area is the flat open ground by the limekilns, over the river from the disused carriage and wagon works building of the Cornwall Railway.

The cause of Lostwithiel's decline as a port, from the mid-14th century onwards, was ironically the cause of its earlier prosperity—tin mining. In the upper reaches of the Fowey the tin-streaming works (there was no deep mining then) deposited large quantities of rubble, sand and soil into the river, which silted up on meeting tidal waters at Lostwithiel, and began to choke the navigable channel. By about 1400 the port had lost nearly all of its trade to the fast-growing port of Fowey, and thereafter the river was restricted to barge traffic only, until even that began to die out at the end of the last century.

Nowadays, the waterborne visitor to Lostwithiel has little time to spare, for fear of being stranded by the falling tide, and must hurry back down the six miles of river to Fowey.

Generations of visitors have delighted in boating on this stretch of the Fowey River, following in the centuries-old wake of the trading vessels, and just one of the many to be captivated by it was Kenneth Grahame whose opening chapter of *The Wind in the Willows*, which is called 'The River Bank', was inspired by a trip upriver to Golant for tea. In this chapter the Water Rat, in conversation with the Mole, gives the most eloquent expression of the water-bound soul: '"And you really live by the river? What a jolly life!" "By it and with it and on it and in it," said the Rat. ". . . It's my world, and I don't want any other. What it hasn't got is not worth having, and what it doesn't know is not worth knowing."'

*The two Looe rivers—'. . . the "A-Roads" of the past . . .'*

# 7 From Polperro to Plymouth Sound

As to the men, one absorbing interest appears to
govern them all. The whole day long they are mend-
ing boats, rowing boats, or standing with their hands
in their pockets, looking at boats.

Looe, from Wilkie Collins, *Rambles Beyond Railways*

## Polperro

PROBABLY Cornwall's most famous fishing harbour, Polperro is the best
example of a village which really must be approached by sea. The usual
land approach is along the main road from Looe which edges down the
valley side to Crumplehorn. This road was new in 1849 and was the focus
of much local pride. It meant that prospective visitors no longer had to
face the terrible hills on the Talland road, or the perils of a sea trip from
Fowey or Plymouth; Polperro was now accessible. Better than anyone,
John Betjeman has described the horrors of the land approach to Polperro
in his *Shell Guide*:

'Coming by the much travelled road from Looe, a cemetery, some
discreet villas and strident petrol stations, then car park succeeding car
park, so that one can hardly notice the valley growing more precipitous,
the enclosing hills more picturesque, for anxiety as to whether the next car

112

park will be full and one will have to turn back—and there is Polperro.' There is no string of car parks now, just one huge one—a tarmacadam monster slouching up the valley, flattening the willows and smothering the stream. It looks like a runway, and it would probably be one if the towering hills did not make an aeronautical approach so hazardous.

So the sea approach is best. Despite everything, Polperro's situation remains breathtaking; crammed into a gleaming gash in the cliffs, houses climbing with an easy arrogance up the sheer valley sides. The harbour itself is narrow and bent, and it is as real and as enigmatic as it should be, and as all working fishing harbours are.

## THE FISHING VILLAGE

Polperro was noted as a fishing community as early as 1303, whereas there was no mention of Mevagissey before 1410. By the 1760's, when John Wesley came to Polperro in the pouring rain, he was left in no doubt that here was a place where fishing was important: 'Here the room over which we were to lodge, being filled with pilchards and conger-eels, the perfume was too potent for me; so that I was not sorry when one of our friends invited me to lodge at her house.'

Two hundred years later, John Betjeman mourned the loss of that old fishing village: 'I can remember Polperro when it smelt of fresh fish instead of fried and had one antique shop, a secondhand bookshop, a few artists' studios and when fishing was still the chief industry.'

Things are not quite as bad now as they were in the 1960s; there are a fairly healthy number of fishing boats in the harbour, a good-smelling fish market on the quay and a famous fishermen's choir (which should definitely not be missed, if the opportunity arises). There is also, as at Mevagissey, that elusive sense of distance between the working life of the harbour and the holiday appeal of the village, and Polperro fishermen are as respected in the Cornish fishing community as they ever were.

The most significant event in Polperro's development, however, was nothing to do with fishing at all. In 1810 the village was discovered by an artist, a member of the Royal Academy called Joseph Farington who arrived by boat and stayed at the Ship Inn. Cornwall was at that time still little visited by artists. Farington wrote that, 'Polperrow is a small fishing port almost wholly inhabited by fishermen . . . Everything that comes into view has a character of simplicity, and is in perfect unison. It is formed for the Landscape Painter.' At the time when Farington was discovering Polperro's quaintness, the village must have been squalid and impoverished. Over 80 years later, when it was thronged with artists enthralled by the picturesque charms of the place, there was an outbreak of typhoid fever. The *West Briton* reported on the appalling living conditions in the village: 'There were no conveniences, and all the excreta, which in typhoid is the most dangerous source of infection, was thrown out of a window into the river, the water of which a little further down was used for washing fish'.

*'. . . it is as real and as enigmatic as it should be . . .'*

## POLPERRO TODAY

Behind the blank and secretive harbour front there is a different Polperro.
There is no denying that this is still an exceptionally attractive place, but
having been made aware of it at such an early stage, it now spoon-feeds its
charms to visitors. The obsession with self-advertisement robs the casual
explorer of any sense of discovery or adventure. The twisted cottages
shout their antiquity at you, flaunt their dates on painted signs, and that
'Olde English' script is everywhere, proclaiming Polperro's connections
with fishing, smuggling, piracy and Jonathon Couch. John Betjeman
wrote that 'the place is more like a new film set than an old Cornish fishing
port'; and in the wonderful book *Turtle Diary* by Russel Hoban, Naera
says of Polperro that 'It was real once but it isn't any more. It's souvenirs
and cream teas and a box with a slot for money to preserve the character of
the old Cornish fishing village . . .'.

There are, of course, still joys to be discovered in Polperro—like
arriving in the harbour on a summer's evening when the pubs are noisy
and friendly, and light spills out into the streets from the open doorways of

114

shops and restaurants, and everywhere there are throngs of people rather than cars. During the day you can always nip up a side street where nobody famous has ever lived, or visit the lovely little church of St John which is cool and white and set a little above the huddle of bent roofs. Best of all is the countryside around Polperro: in almost every direction there is somewhere wonderful to explore in order to restore faith in your own initiative.

## TOWARDS LANSALLOS

The harbour's craggy guardian rock, with the restored sail-loft sheltering against it, is called the Peak; and above it there is Chapel Cliff, taking its name from the medieval chapel of St Peter (the patron saint of fishermen) which used to stand high on the cliff, protecting the infant harbour.

A little further on along the coastal path the ruins of fish-drying houses crouch in the undergrowth which spills with abandon down the hillside. The stretch of coastline from here to Polruan, most of which is owned by the National Trust, is glorious. Lansallos, an ancient holy place set in folded fields above Lantivet Bay, is not far from here along the switch-back coastal path and then up the old sand way from the beach through West Coombe.

## TO TALLAND

In the other direction, Talland is even nearer. You can walk there along the coast path or take the old road out of Polperro up Talland Hill. In 1871 Jonathon Couch wrote that 'The new road was cut in 1849, and is so important to the traffic of the town that the stranger who misses his way and descends on horseback the old Talland road, if he has time to spare on any subject than the safety of himself and horse, will be puzzled to conceive how we contrived to do so long without it'. The disconcerting thing about the gruelling climb up Talland Hill is that at the point of exhaustion, with legs like sacks of wet sand, you are quite likely to be overtaken by a group of Polperro octogenarians, steaming effortlessly up the desperate incline and chattering all the way.

From the top of Sand Hill, looking down into Talland Bay, it is hard at first to pick out Talland Church; it perches, with the old barton farm, a little way up the far hill, and has the confusing backdrop of a field full of caravans. That is just about the only jarring element here; down in the bay there is a small grassy car park, a hut selling tea and little else. Further on is Rotterdam, just below the church, where there used to be a corn mill, washed into the sea about 200 years ago.

## INLAND FROM POLPERRO

The parishes of Lansallos, Pelynt, Lanteglos, St Veep and Lanreath make up one of Cornwall's enchanted corners. The lanes meander anarchically about between towering hedges, taking the occasional sickening plunge into a tiny willow-filled valley. This is Geoffrey Grigson country, and anyone who wants to know more about the area, and to fall in love with it, should read his wonderful *Freedom of the Parish* which he described as 'an act of loyalty or *pietas* to my first biological territory . . . one man's version of a tract of land, one man's story of the freedom of his parish which he gained by the accident and privilege of birth and upbringing within its borders.'

## Looe

Looe is not seen at its best from the sea, despite the dramatic introduction provided by the great green swell of Looe Island which breaks surface just to the south of the harbour.

Neither East nor West Looe has ever looked out to sea; the houses and port buildings all look inwards upon the river that has given Looe its prosperity. Harper wrote in 1910 that 'The life of the Looes, East and West, is all along the streets and quays beside the estuary', and this is still true today. The streets are full of life and charm while the sea front is incoherent and soulless; the old lifeboat house is the only interesting building on the East Looe side.

The church looks strangely out of place, but there is no particular reason why it should: the tower is old (it used to be whitewashed as a seamark), and even if the church body only dates from 1883, the site is that of a chapel of St Mary first dedicated in 1259.

The sea walls and Banjo Pier have been Looe's little promenade since they were built early in the last century (although the round end to the pier, and thus its name, did not come to be until 1896). 'Here the idlers of the place assemble to lounge and gossip', Wilkie Collins observed in 1852, 'to look out for any outward-bound ships that are to be seen in the Channel, and to criticise the appearance and glorify the capabilities of the little fleet of Looe fishing-boats, riding snugly at anchor before them at the entrance of the bay.'

On the west side of the river mouth beneath the towering hotels is the gloomy and magnificent Hannafore road with its arches and turrets, which was built by the noted engineer and local benefactor Joseph Thomas and opened, with great celebrations, in 1895.

### THE TWO LOOES

West Looe was originally called Portbuan or Portbyghan, meaning 'small harbour', and its old heart, the one street climbing up the valley towards Portlooe, is still quiet and simple in comparison with its bustling neighbour across the river. It is the combination of the two, the contrasts and the complementary charms, which draws travellers and visitors to Looe again and again, and has done so for centuries.

In 1724, Daniel Defoe came here as part of his tour of Britain and commented that the Looes were 'both good trading towns', but had to conclude that 'as to sending four members to the British Parliament (which is as many as the City of London chooses), that, I confess, seems a little scandalous.' This extraordinary situation lasted until 1832, when the Great Reform Act was passed. During the debates on the rotten boroughs and parliamentary reform which preceded this bill, one MP declared that 'There is only one borough more rotten than East Looe and that is West Looe.'

Defoe also mentioned the 'beautiful and stately stone bridge' joining the two boroughs, as did most other visitors to Looe. That bridge is not the one which stands today. It was a 'great Bridg' (according to Leland) which had about fifteen arches (descriptions differ) and square openings at either end for the passage of barges. Being under construction in 1411, it was thus the oldest of the four great estuary bridges of Devon and Cornwall; the others being Bideford (about 1459), Barnstaple (1437) and Wadebridge (1470). A chapel on the bridge dedicated to St Anne was probably destroyed during the Reformation. The road carried was the ancient coast road, the same one that crosses the Fowey at Bodinnick and the Fal at King Harry Ferry.

For much of the 19th century, increased traffic on the old bridge was causing concern and this is largely why it was replaced. Its position, about 100 yards downriver from the new one, is marked on the West Looe bank by a granite tablet in the wall below the helpfully named Old Bridge House, which records that the bridge was 'Repeared by the County 1689'. Sadly, the ancient structure was not retained as a monument, the reason being, according to Jonathon Couch, that the Admiralty required it to be demolished 'to allow of larger accommodation for the increase in shipping, which has followed the prosperity of mines near Liskeard'.

The writer Wilkie Collins was a visitor to Looe in 1852, just before the bridge's demolition. He stayed for some time and was obviously taken with the place, describing it at some length in *Rambles Beyond Railways*.

When the time came to leave, he experienced that old Cornish affliction which gets to most people in the end—a great difficulty in getting going: 'Even when we had made our determination and fixed our farewell day, a great boat-race and a great tea-drinking, which everybody declared was something that everybody else ought to see, interfered to detain us.' What better reasons to postpone departure could there have been?

The 'mazes of little narrow streets' which Wilkie found in East Looe are still surprisingly enchanting. Despite the odd outbreak of 'Olde English' script, most of the houses are closed and secretive, and there are tiny back-alleys crammed with dustbins, flower pots, flights of stone steps and faded double yellow lines which meet in the middle. Above all, wherever you go there are boats: boats lurk in garages (the cars in Looe know their proper place), hang upside-down from rafters, and squeeze into every possible doorway and warehouse. Look out also for the old guildhall which dates from about 1500 and now houses a fine little museum.

## THE QUAYS

Down on the quays you will no longer see the throng of coasting vessels which Wilkie described and it is hard to guess that Looe was once one of the busiest ports in the Southwest, until competition from Plymouth and Fowey after the 14th century proved too much.

In the last century, after hundreds of years in the doldrums, Looe experienced a renaissance and became the main outlet for the rich mining area to the north of Liskeard. A canal was first built to link the port with Moorswater in Liskeard, and replaced with the railway in December 1860. Moorswater was the terminus for a network of railways serving the great copper mines and granite quarries to the north. The new rail link increased the tonnage of goods reaching Looe by quite a margin: in 1858, for instance, the canal carried 44,504 tons while the railway, five years later, carried 62,212 tons. The problem then was that Looe did not have enough wharfage to cope with the increased trade. In 1861 it was reported that over £4000 worth of copper ore was lying unshipped on the quays, and at times there were as many as 30 ships waiting to load or discharge. The congestion was relieved to some extent in the 1860s when the quays were lengthened seawards.

Reconstruction work on the lower quay wall has only recently been completed, but this time the work was undertaken for the fishing fleet which is keeping Looe's quays and harbourside industries alive, and which is now looking larger and healthier than it has done for many years.

## UP THE HANNAFORE ROAD

Just at the beginning of the Hannafore road in West Looe is the little church of St Nicholas, the patron saint of sailors, which was endowed before 1330 and in its career has served as a guildhall, prison, law court, polling booth and school. It was eventually returned to its proper use in 1852.

From here onwards, Joseph Thomas's creation takes off under the dark cliffs and perching hotels around to Hannafore which feels like a place abroad. There is something particularly foreign about the low and gentle shore shelving out towards Looe Island. The island is one of the many places in Cornwall which claims to have been the landing place for Joseph of Arimathea and the young Jesus on their way to Glastonbury. Although privately owned, visitors are welcomed ashore in the summer by the two Atkins sisters, whose remarkable story is told in *We Bought an Island* and *Tales from our Cornish Island*.

There are the ruins of a small chapel on the island that had belonged to the monastery or cell of Lammana on the mainland. The last house on the Hannafore road, before it becomes a footpath, is called Monk's House, and there in the garden is a splendid piece of walling incorporating two window slits, all that remains of the monastic living quarters of that Celtic cell. The low walls of another chapel can be found a little further on, and higher up the hill, protected by a wooden fence. Evidence newly uncovered shows that this chapel is a later, medieval, development, its position being both safer and more convenient for the resident monks and visiting pilgrims than that of the original Celtic chapel on the island. Both chapels were dedicated to St Michael, who was often the patron of churches in lofty and commanding situations; there used to be chapels with this dedication on Roughtor (one of only two mountains in Cornwall), Roche Rock, Rame Head and of course St Michael's Mount.

## THE TWO LOOE RIVERS

The name Looe means pool (or in this case probably creek or tidal pool) in Cornish. As there are two towns, so there are two rivers, East and West, and the parish between them is called Duloe, 'two pools'. They are not major rivers like the Fowey and the Fal, but they were still the A Roads of the past, and in a boat of shallow draft you can still travel quite a way up both of them.

Alternatively, to see something of the East Looe valley you can take the train to Liskeard which trundles slowly up through the wildland with the steep and secret valley sides rising on either side of the track. Like the branch line from Par to Newquay (which takes you up through the tumbling Luxulyan Valley and across the Goss Moor), this line travels through some wonderful country, and has the added advantage of the unintentional charm of Liskeard—an old market town which retains all of its ancestral vibrancy on market days—as its destination. On the way you will pass Sandplace, the highest point to be reached by the tide on the East Looe. The name refers to the sea sand from Looe which was landed here from earliest times, for the inland farmers to spread on their acid soils. Many other cargoes used to be barged up to Sandplace, especially limestone which was burned in the many limekilns here (some are now converted, others overgrown and crumbling) from the 18th century onwards, and then also used as a fertilizer.

When standing on the station platform at Looe, with Shutta (said by some to be the earliest inhabited part of East Looe) behind you, the West Looe River beckons from beyond Trenant Point. It is another world from the noisy, crowded streets of Looe; a secret wooded invitation which it is impossible to ignore. Thomas Bond in his 1823 *History of East and West Looe* reminds us that this has long been a popular place for Looe people to go walking: 'There is . . . a most delightful walk or ride along the banks of the Western River, in a fine coppice wood, for two miles up. Now and then you are entertained with the notes and a view of the heron, the seagull, the curlew, the woodpecker, and sylvan doves; and the kingfisher, as if to shew its beautiful plumage, frequently flits from the rock below, and skims along before you.'

In Bond's time holiday-makers used to boat up to Watergate, where the woodland path emerges on to the road, to sit in the public fruit gardens and eat cream and syllabubs made from cider, milk and sugar. Watergate today is a peaceful little pocket overshadowed by the steep wooded hills which rise up all about it. A little way up the lane which runs alongside the river up to Sowden's Bridge you will come upon the riotously overgrown limekilns at Shallowpool and, on the other side of the road, the jungly old wharves on the riverbank where the coal and limestone, and for centuries before that the sea sand and weed, used to be unloaded from the tidal barges. About 200 yards before the kilns there is the entrance to an old sunken green lane which heads up through the woods; this was the way from the important medieval manor of Trelawne down to the river—its lifeline to the outside world.

## Portwrinkle

Halfway along the bald sweep of Whitsand Bay, beyond the rambling Downderry, the once industrious fishing village of Portwrinkle huddles on the low clifftop. If offers no invitation to mariners today, but it still has the remains of its old curving harbour wall, made from huge lumps of rock and looking as though it had just risen from the sea, with a new breakwater built within it. The old pier was largely destroyed by a storm on February 2, 1882.

Hard as it is to imagine any boats in the harbour, Edward Kneebone described it in 1684 as 'a large fisher Towne, having an Excellent Key or Mould, Standing the Rage of the South Sea, Sufficient to Secure all their Boats, and good large Barks upon occasions'.

### THE PILCHARD FISHERY

Portwrinkle is a settlement planned deliberately to take advantage of the pilchard fishing industry which was expanding and becoming better organized, in Tudor and Stuart times. There have been similar schemes throughout history; in this century, for instance, one of Lord Leverhulme's projects was to transform the village of Obbe on Harris in the Outer Hebrides into a thriving herring port. The new settlement kept its new name of Leverburgh but it never found prosperity, and was never quite completed by Leverhulme. Portwrinkle could easily have become, like Leverburgh, a sad place echoing with the dreams of dead men, for it too had all its eggs in that one unreliable basket, but there has been enough farming and tourism, in particular, to keep the place alive. The tourist industry has yet to spoil Portwrinkle; its most noticeable effect is the wonderfully eccentric Whitsand Bay Hotel which began life as a private house in Torpoint but in 1909 was removed brick by brick from its original site and rebuilt here.

Portwrinkle's history is whispered by more than the megalithic harbour alone; up on the hillside to the west of the village, for instance, there are two square leading-lights in which fires used to be lit to guide the fishing boats into harbour at night. Then there are the pilchard cellars unmistakable and magnificent by the roadside. The pilchard fishery was such that it generated other industries and created a thriving community. The waste products of the bulking process, when the pilchards were stacked in the cellars between layers of salt and left to compress and drain, had a variety of uses: the oil ('train oil' as it was called) was primarily used

*'It offers no invitation to mariners today'*

for lighting, and the blood and brine ('the drugs') was spread on the land as fertilizer. Portwrinkle would also have had its own cooperage to make the 20–40,000 hogsheads needed each season, not to mention the casks needed for the oil and drugs. As with harvest-time on land, when (and if) the pilchard shoals arrived off the coast the whole community would be involved. Bulking, compressing and packing were generally carried out by women and children while the men were involved in catching and carrying the fish.

Everything depended upon the pilchard; and as that capricious fish began inexplicably to disappear from these waters and the industry moved further and further west, so the whole community crumbled. The three foundations of Cornwall's prosperity—tin, copper, and pilchards—all failed in the last years of the 19th century, with catastrophic effects throughout the county.

## Cawsand Bay

Beyond Rame Head and Penlee Point the huge un-Cornish grandeur of Plymouth Sound unrolls before you. On the western edge of the Sound, embraced by the arboreal arms of Mount Edgcumbe, is the deep water of Cawsand Bay which for centuries has sheltered whole fleets of ships from all but southeasterly gales. Those can be devastating, as in January 1817 when a particular gale caused damage costing upwards of £5,000. The *West Briton* reported that 'one house, with a man who dwelt in it, was completely swept away'. In general, however, the bay is a natural haven and, as John Betjeman described it, 'a complete tropical contrast with the bleakness of Whitsand Bay on the other side of Rame Head'.

There is no harbour here as such, but the bay was always the chief anchorage for ships in the Sound until the breakwater was built in the early 19th century. Fleets gathered here before setting off on voyages of trade or exploration or war. In 1583 Edward Hayes, who was to sail with Sir Humphrey Gilbert to Newfoundland, wrote in his diary on Tuesday, June 11 that 'The last place of our assembly, before we left the west of England, was in Causet Bay neere unto Plimouth'. Likewise, it was from Cawsand Bay that Sir Francis Drake and Sir John Hawkins set out on Friday, August 29, 1595 on their final voyage to the West Indies, with 27 ships and 2,500 men and boys.

## KINGSAND AND CAWSAND

On the shore of the bay are the two villages of Kingsand and Cawsand, which for most of their history were not only in different parishes but actually in different counties. All that separates them is a tiny stream, and idle visitors will find no distinction at all between the two places, but that sliver of water was for a time a national boundary between Celtic Cornwall and Saxon England.

It seems incredible now to think that there was ever a time when the Tamar River was not the boundary here, but it was not until 1844 that Kingsand and Mount Edgcumbe were given back to Cornwall. In all but name they must have been a part of Cornwall all that time, however, despite the traditional enmity between the two villages. Betjeman considered that Kingsand 'still has a look . . . of a Devon fishing village'; that may be, but it has the *feel* of Cornwall. Neither village could be anywhere but in Cornwall. True, there is a special remoteness about the Rame Peninsula—it is like nowhere else in the county—but the same can also be said of the Lizard or West Penwith or the Roseland: they are all places which have somehow been bypassed by the scurry of progress. The genuine friendliness to be found here in the Rame Peninsula, along with the unconscious charm of the villages and the grandeur of the scenery, is enough to make this little land stand out above anywhere else in Cornwall.

There is an unusual number of old pilchard cellars around the bay, most of which were built by opportunists in the 1580s in an attempt to cut out the Plymouth middlemen. There are several along the shore from Kingsand towards the semicircular fort (now converted into flats) at Picklecombe Point. One 'palace' is in good condition and will hopefully remain as a store for local fishermen rather than fall into the hands of developers. The others are in varying stages of decay, some in use as stores, others just tumbled walls. They are built between the cliffs and the broad, dusty-pink rock platform from which stone was cut for their construction. The gaps made by these excavations became 'false coves', providing artificial passages through the rock for the fish-laden boats; some of them, such as Martin's Cove and Mallard's Cove, might well have

*Kingsand—'. . . the bay is a natural haven'*

been named after the pioneers of such a practice. By the furthest cellars, at
Sandway, there used to be a Bark House (there were four originally in the
area) where oak bark was boiled and the solution used to preserve the seine
nets.

Above the cellars, the bracken, gorse and stubby trees rise to the ivy-
grown walls of a fort. There are many fortifications, old and new, all over
the Rame Peninsula, leaving no-one in any doubt as to the area's strategic
importance in the defence of Plymouth; wherever you turn old walls are
watching.

In the centuries following the building of the cellars, smuggling as well
as fishing flourished in Cawsand Bay. The 'free trade' was at its height
during the 18th and early 19th centuries, and Cawsand Bay became the
unofficial headquarters of West Country smuggling operations (yet you
would hardly guess it for the lack of 'ye olde smugglers' cafés and shops).
In 1804 the chief Customs officer of Plymouth estimated that an average of
17,000 casks of spirits were smuggled into the two villages every year and
fifty smuggling craft were said to be based in the bay. Five years earlier,
George Lipscombe had a strange encounter during his *Journey into
Cornwall*:

'In going down the hill, towards Kingsand, we met several females,
whose appearance was so grotesque and extraordinary, that I could not
imagine in what manner they had contrived to alter their natural shapes so
completely; till, upon enquiry, we found that they were smugglers of
spiritous liquors; which they were at that time conveying from their cutter
to Plymouth by means of bladders fastened under their petticoats; and,
indeed, they were so heavily laden that it was with great apparent
difficulty they waddled along.'

123

## TO RAME HEAD AND RAME CHURCH

The walk from Cawsand to Rame Head is outstanding; along the way you see all the various and complementary faces of Cornwall. From Penlee Point, where you emerge from the luxuriance of the woods on to the wild russet cliffs which stretch away to Rame Head, there is a dramatic view across the Sound.

Prominent in the Sound is the Breakwater which made such a difference to the development of Plymouth, and to the Naval Dockyard at Devonport in particular. The plans for its construction were drawn up by the celebrated engineer John Rennie and adopted in 1811. The breakwater could not be connected to the land on either side of the Sound because it would have created a trap for the huge quantities of silt carried down by the Tamar and Plym Rivers. Construction was problematical and hazardous and took nearly 30 years: it was not finished until 1841.

Across the narrow neck of Rame Head, between dizzying precipices, run the ancient bulwarks of a cliff castle which fortified the point, like the Dodman, in the Iron Age. Mounting the last few steps to the chapel (even in a light wind this is fairly hair-raising) is like coming to the end of a pilgrimage; the chapel is a place of great stillness and tranquillity, despite its position. It was built with massive walls of local stone in the 14th century on the probable site of a Celtic hermitage. The small window high up in the west wall, through which the sun slants onto old stone, suggests that it must once have had an upper room, possibly a hermit's cell. As well as being a sacred site, Rame Head has long been an important seamark (St Michael's Chapel making the headland especially distinctive) and lookout point. As early as 1486 there is a record of the town of Plymouth paying a watchman to maintain a beacon here to warn shipping, and to bring news to Plymouth of such horrors as Barbary corsairs, Breton pirates and Dutch privateers, as well as good news like the return of the Newfoundland fishing fleet in 1543.

From Rame, the contrast between the cliffs back to Penlee Point on one side and the sweep of Whitsand Bay on the other could not be more marked. Much of the latter's severe beauty has been ruined by the holiday chalets running riot at Tregonhawke and Wiggle. The cliffs look as though they have caught a particularly nasty disease; let us hope that it is not contagious.

Inland from Rame Head and past the Coastguard station, you will soon come upon a little oasis of life gathered about Rame Church. This rough slate church with its simple spire and rectangular sanctuary, finding some shelter in its desolate position, must be one of the finest in Cornwall.

# 8 The Tamar and Lynher Rivers

Either shore
Presents its combinations to the view
Of all that interests, delights, enchants:
Corn-waving fields, and pastures fair, and slope
And swell alternate, summits crowned with leaf,
And grove-encircled mansions, verdant capes,
The beach, the inn, the farm, the mill, the path,
And tinkling rivulets, and waters wide
Presenting here the semblance of a lake,
There, winding round some unexpected point,
Now shut, now open. Nor is wanting oft,
Dotting the wandering flood, the varying sail
Of barge, or fishing-bark, or painted skiff
Of joyous voyagers.

H. E. Carrington, from his *Guide to Plymouth and Devonport
with Sketches of the Surrounding Scenery* (1837)

THE two rivers, the Tamar and the Lynher, join and pour into Plymouth
Sound through the most slender of funnels, where Devon and Cornwall
almost touch, called the Narrows. The extraordinary contrast here
between the bold, sylvan beauty of Mount Edgcumbe on the one hand,
and the seething mass of Plymouth (Stonehouse, to be exact) just 300
yards away across the water, is echoed all the way up the Tamar, where the
ever-contrasting banks lend a unique asymmetrical beauty to this great
border river.

## Cremyll and Mount Edgcumbe

One of the Tamar's oldest crossing points is at Cremyll, and the passage is mentioned in documents as far back as 1250 though it is probably considerably older, being the main link with Cornwall on the ancient coastal highway. In the centuries before Plymouth Breakwater was built this crossing could be extremely dangerous, and many travellers have written of their alarming voyages across this short stretch of water. The intrepid Celia Fiennes who rode *Through England on a Side-Saddle* in 1695 considered 'Cribly Ferry' to be 'a very hazardous passage by reason of three tides meeting', and the crossing took her at least an hour.

On the far side of the water from Cremyll's cluster of cottages are the grand old buildings of the Royal William Victualling Yard, built by Rennie at much the same time as his Breakwater. Despite its proud maritime past, Plymouth as a city has largely turned its back on the sea. The exceptions are the Barbican and Sutton Harbour, where fishing boats mingle with yachts and pleasure steamers and where the fresh smell of fish lurks around the fashionable little shops and Elizabethan houses; the Hoe where you can stand by Smeaton's old Eddystone Lighthouse and look out across the Sound to Drake's Island and the woods of Mount Edgcumbe; and of course Devonport Dockyard, a great maritime city in itself.

Cremyll today is famous for its popular old passage inn the Edgcumbe Arms, and for Mashfords Yard, a shipyard of great renown on a site hollowed out of the hill, where boatbuilding has been carried on continuously for at least 200 years. The main use for the ferry these days is in transporting the people of Plymouth to and from Mount Edgcumbe Country Park. The 865 acre park, which is open from 8 in the morning until dusk every day, at no charge, was bought for the people of Cornwall and Plymouth by their councils in 1970. The glorious grounds include a Tudor deer park, acres of woodland, a series of formal and landscaped gardens and ten miles of wonderful coastline. The house itself was completely rebuilt in its original style when the old 16th century mansion was destroyed by German incendiary bombs in 1941.

There can be few estates in Britain to have received as much adoration and admiration as has Mount Edgcumbe. The 18th century actor David Garrick wrote an ode to Mount Edgcumbe in which he declared that 'This mount all the mounts of England surpasses'; Queen Victoria loved the chestnut trees; and Celia Fiennes considered it the finest seat she had ever seen. Josiah Wedgwood, on his first visit to explore the china clay district, wrote in a letter from Plymouth: 'We were upon the waters several hours yesterday afternoon. Have you seen Mount Edgcumbe? If you have not seen Mount Edgcumbe you have seen nothing. We sailed twice past this terrestrial paradise, and such a sun setting I never beheld.'

As well as praising it, people have always coveted Mount Edgcumbe. The Duke of Medina Sidonia is reputed to have been so infatuated that it was to have been his reward had the Spanish Armada of 1588, of which he was the commander, been successful.

'. . . "lurketh between two hills" . . .'

## Millbrook

Under the steep green bluff of Clarrick and Pigshill Woods with the tower of Maker Church above, Millbrook Lake idles westwards past the stump of an old windmill at Empacombe, and past one lovely cottage after another, placid by the water's edge. In Leland's day Millbrook was 'a riche Fischar Toun', and Carew remembered that the village, which 'lurketh between two hills', 'took great increase of wealth and buildings through the just and industrious trade of fishing, and had wellnear 40 ships and barks at one time belonging thereunto'.

The old part of Millbrook still has the confusing street pattern of a typical Cornish fishing village, but it no longer has any sea. The old limekilns and the town quay now stand on a new lake formed as part of a flood prevention scheme, cutting Millbrook off from the tidal estuary; and the businesses on the quay, once bark houses, net lofts and fish cellars, are now devoted to the motor car. The former millpond which occupied a northern bulge of the creek has been filled in to make a recreation area, but some of the old buildings of the Insworke tide mill remain at the southeast corner. A little downstream at Anderton, on the south bank opposite Foss, a fine strong wall surrounds what was once an important boatyard. The line of the old ropewalk can still be made out leaving the road just past the yard. Ships for the Black Prince are reputed to have been built here.

Today, Millbrook bristles with industrial remains and modern residential development (many Millbrook people work across the water in the Dockyard), but a century ago this was a booming industrial centre in its own right.

127

Most of Millbrook's industry was concentrated at Foss and Southdown on the low near-island beyond Insworke (the name Insworke includes the Cornish enys, meaning 'island'). At Southdown a gunpowder mill had existed since at least 1650 (it blew up in 1850), and later industries crowding about the quay included a soap factory, glue works, fish fertilizer plant, the Southdown Metal & Chemical Company, and the Southdown Brick Works. Perhaps the most interesting of Southdown's industries was the King's Brewhouse (including a cooperage, malthouse and dwellings) which brewed beer for the Royal Navy for 150 years. There is little to be seen today of the brewery or any of the other Southdown industries; despite some activity around the quay, this is a strange echoing place with ivy-grown ruins everywhere—just anonymous shapes in the undergrowth—and piles of broken bricks.

## St John's Lake

This wide and shallow expanse of water has the cream-and-chocolate block buildings of HMS *Raleigh* and HMS *Fisgard* and the colourless rows of Torpoint on its northern shore. Torpoint owes its existence to the ferry which was established in 1791, and to the new road built to meet it. In 1835 it became a 'floating bridge' ferry, like King Harry, and remained the primary crossing into Cornwall until the Tamar road bridge was built at Saltash in 1961. The ferries are rather grand, like huge river monsters passing midstream, and are still a vital link for those Plymouth workers who live in the Torpoint area. The ugly waterfront at Torpoint is partially redeemed by a splendid 18th century warehouse, recently renovated, and by the large 1783 Ballast Pound now used for moorings.

The little village of St John, scattered among orchards and streams at the hilly head of the creek, seems doubly green and lost in contrast with the dramatic view of the docks with their cranes, huge frigate-refitting sheds and warehouses, their tower blocks and dignified old dockyard buildings. At St John there is a charming, stubby little church, an inn, a large number of converging lanes, and not enough new buildings to destroy the peaceful, cloistered atmosphere.

The Hamoaze is that deep stretch of water between the Narrows and the confluence of the Tamar and Lynher Rivers. Norden wrote in 1584 that it was 'a saufe and comodious Roade for Shippinge', and so it was in 1691 when William III began to build his Royal Naval Dockyard on its Devon bank, and so it remains today for yachts and dinghies as well as for the sleek, grey naval vessels and the shadowy figures of nuclear submarines.

There is still a serious threat hanging over the peaceful shores of St John's Lake, for the Insworke peninsula is one of the sites favoured by the CEGB for a new coal-fired power station. It could have a capacity of anything up to 2000 megawatts and burn over 4 million tonnes of coal per annum, some of which would be shipped in 40,000 tonne vessels, but most would be brought in via a new railhead around the shore of St John's Lake from Saltash. Quite apart from the power station buildings themselves, the area would have to support storage space for coal and slag, new road and rail links, new transmission lines running north to Landulph, temporary labour camps, new housing estates, a huge increase in the traffic load: no matter what the safeguards, the effects on the incomparable Rame Peninsula would be overwhelming and devastating.

## The River Lynher

The Lynher used to be navigable up to Notter Bridge, and its tributary the Tiddy up as far as Tideford, but these days it is inadvisable to venture much further than St Germans on the Tiddy and the boatyard at Treluggan on the Lynher, and then only on good high tides.

The ferry which used to run between Jupiter Point on the Antony estate and Antony Passage on the north bank of the Lynher was an ancient crossing belonging to the manor of East Antony (Antony as it is now) and mentioned as early as 1324. Antony House, the ancestral home of the Carew family and still lived in by their descendents, is now owned by the National Trust; along with its extensive grounds it is open to the public on Tuesdays, Wednesdays and Thursdays in the summer months.

The hamlet of Antony Passage is dominated by the old tide mill (its pond walls still intact but its four massive waterwheels gone), by a viaduct carrying the main line over Forder Lake, and by the great Norman castle of Trematon which has been owned by the Earldom and then the Duchy of Cornwall since 1275. It is Leland's 'round Castel of the Kinges . . . a great and auncient Castelle apon a Rokky Hille, whereof great Peaces yet stond and especially the Dungeon'.

Ince Castle stands on a low promontory a little upriver from Antony Passage. More than 400 years younger than Trematon, Ince was Cornwall's first great brick house, built for the Killigrew family in the 16th century.

## WACKER QUAY

As the Lynher turns from the low, chequered arable land to the north and dives south to squeeze around the foot of Earth Hill, it passes the wooded Warren Point and the entrance to Wacker Lake. Wacker Quay, sandwiched between the tidal waters and the new road to Torpoint, is now a picnic area and cars park on the water's edge.

Less than a century ago its role was rather different. It was built in the 19th century, replacing an earlier quay which had served Wacker tide mill (which no longer exists). A tramway and cable-incline were constructed from the quay inland, to carry loads of Gunnislake granite to build the forts of Scraesdon on the hill above Wacker Quay, and Tregantle on the coast above Whitsand Bay. Palmerston, while Prime Minister in the mid-19th century, was obsessed with the belief that the French were going to attack Devonport Dockyard, so a number of these huge solid forts were built on his orders on the high land around Plymouth Sound.

In the later part of the century the tramway was converted to a railway to carry the heavy nine-inch shells for the Tregantle Ordnance, as well as water and other supplies for the garrisons. The railway ceased to be used in 1904 but the rails were not taken up until 1916. The old locomotive shed is still there on Wacker Quay, and you can still make out the line of the cable-incline, with its gradient of 1 in 7 heading uphill to Scraesdon on the right of the new road, halfway between Wacker Quay and the churchtown of Antony.

## EARTH PASSAGE

Around the corner from Wacker, the Lynher is a peaceful lake caught between the bold swell of Earth Hill (sometimes 'Erth') and the Sheviock Woods on the western bank. These woods (not yet entirely safe from the threat of destruction or a complete coniferous takeover) are recorded in the Domesday Book of 1086 and, over the centuries, have provided everything from cover for smugglers to wood for houses, fences and fuel. Down on the shore, at the foot of a slight valley, was George's Quay. All that remains now is an old, tumbled green lane leading straight back up through the woods to the lovely churchtown of Sheviock, a relic of the time when it was Sheviock's main link with the outside world and when the Lynher was not the still and solitary waterway it is today.

The powerful canons of St Germans Priory had their wood barged upriver from George's Quay from earliest times, and the lords of Sheviock used to give the canons two barge-loads of wood a year until 1260, when the then lord put an end to the custom by giving them fifteen acres of his woodland. Directly across the river from George's Quay are the remains of Earth Quay, which was not just a manorial landing-place for Earth Barton (slightly upriver and around the hill) but the other end of an ancient lost ford and ferry passage across the Lynher. There is evidence that this crossing was in common use in the past; the diary of William Carnsew, for instance, relates that in September 1577 he 'came to Arthe' and then, the following day, 'paste the Water' and 'went to Sheviocke cherche'.

The faintest shadow of a causeway can sometimes be made out at low tide, with imagination, but little else remains of a crossing or of a quay at the end of George's Lane.

## St Germans

Leland wrote in the 1540s that 'St Germane's is but a poor Fischar Town; the Glory of it stoode by the Priory of Blake Canons, and a Paroche Chirche yn the Body of the Same'. Almost nothing remains today of the priory; the fine house of Port Eliot, still the home of the Eliot family, stands on the site of the old priory buildings, most of which fell into decay after its dissolution. The gardens and grounds of Port Eliot were laid out by Humphrey Repton in 1792, an operation which even included the diversion of the Tiddy in order to make The Lawn.

The church does remain, however, and anything less like a Cornish parish church is hard to imagine. Despite its self-effacing position in a hollow, the church is magnificent. The west front, with its two towers and wonderful doorway (to which centuries of storms have given great weathered weals and the everlasting impression of dashing headlong into the wind) is pure Norman work, started before 1185. The village of St Germans might seem an unusual setting for such a huge and ancient church; but this parish is still the largest in Cornwall and the predecessor to this Norman church was Cornwall's cathedral from 926, when King Athelstan made Conan the first Cornish Bishop, until 1043 when the see was transferred to Crediton, and thence to Exeter in 1050. From then until 1876, when the Bishopric of Truro was established, the Church in Cornwall was controlled from the capital of Devon.

## THE QUAY

St Germans Quay is a sturdy construction with a few floral cottages and old warehouses, a sailing club, and ruined limekilns which lurk under the trees in the shadow of the railway viaduct. Like most river quays its heyday came in the last century with cargoes of tin, copper and lead to be loaded and coal, timber and limestone to be landed. From the middle of the century until the 1930s there was also a ferry service between St Germans and Devonport on market days, calling at all the small quays en route (George's, Wacker, Tredown, Clift, Bullard, Wearde etc) to collect soft fruit, vegetables and passengers.

Between the wars, when river traffic everywhere was beginning to die out, the Lynher was kept alive by a vigorous trade in blue elvan road stone which was shipped downstream in sailing barges (the *Shamrock* at Cotehele Quay used to work the Lynher) from the quarries at Treluggan and Poldrissick, above the confluence with the Tiddy, and from Forder by Antony Passage. Ironically these cargoes of stone built the roads which put an end to the working life of the river.

Just to the south of St Germans Quay, Polbathick Lake, which was formerly navigable up to the village of Polbathick with its limekilns and roadside pub, skirts around the bottom of the worst housing in Cornwall, the new St Germans.

## Saltash

This is the Saltash that Daniel Defoe found in 1724: 'From Plymouth we pass the Tamar over a ferry to Saltash—a little poor, shattered town, the first we set foot on in the county of Cornwall. The Tamar here is very wide, and the ferry-boats bad; so that I thought myself well escaped when I got safe on shore in Cornwall. Saltash seems to be the ruins of a larger place; and we saw many houses, as it were, falling down, and I doubt not that the mice and rats have abandoned many more, as they say they will when they are likely to fall. Yet this town is governed by a mayor and

*'". . . The only light on shore gleamed from the tavern window . . ."'*

aldermen, has many privileges, sends members to Parliament, takes toll of all vessels that pass the river, and has the sole oyster-fishing in the whole river, which is considerable.'

This strange state of affairs was just the faint echo of a time when Saltash was the foremost seaport between Dartmouth and Fowey, a position based on the export of tin but held for less than a century, because by 1260 Plymouth had already eclipsed its older neighbour. The Saltash ferry, no longer needed once the road bridge was built, was known as Ash-Torre Passage and was, with Cremyll, the oldest and most important ferry crossing in Cornwall.

From most angles Saltash is a drab place and a sorry gateway to Cornwall, but in the little streets running down to the waterfront, under the shadow of the two great bridges, something of the old Saltash lingers. There are still pubs down on the quays, as there were when Wilkie Collins was brought here, on a slight diversion, by his boatman, a bibulous rascal called William Dawle: 'There was no mistaking the tavern. The only light on shore gleamed from the tavern window; and, judging by the criterion of noise, the whole local population seemed to be collected within the tavern walls. We opened the door; and found ourselves in a small room, filled with shrimpers, sailors, fishermen and watermen, all "looming large" through a fog of tobacco, and all chirping merrily over their cups.'

Since 1859, however, it has been hard to notice Saltash at all because the scene is so dominated by Brunel's Royal Albert Bridge. Brunel's first plan to cross the Tamar, drawn up in 1846, was for a steam train ferry to run on the same route as the ancient passenger ferry, but under the act of Parliament the Cornish Railway was only allowed to cross the river here on a bridge. His next two ideas, for a double-track timber bridge of seven spans, and one of four spans, were both rejected by the Admiralty who demanded a minimum height of 100 feet above high water and no more than one pier. It was a tall order, but Brunel went on to design his single-track wrought iron bridge, and caused quite a stir. The *West Briton*, having compared the size of the proposed bridge with various Cornish landmarks, concluded: 'Fancy, then, these two enormous arches built on the top of a pier nearly twice as high as Truro spire; and then imagine railroad carriages dashing on at railroad pace over this terrific structure!'

Brunel was unable to attend the official opening of his fabulous beast, which was to end forever Cornwall's ancient isolation, on May 2, 1859 because he was in Rome and too ill to travel. Later that month he was able to make it back, and was drawn slowly across the bridge on a couch mounted on a flat truck; he died four months later.

## Kingsmill Lake

Opposite Devon's Tamerton Lake and the wooded Warleigh Point, Kingsmill Lake wanders for quite a distance into remote farmland, and was once crowded with barge traffic and dotted with small farm quays. Moditonham Quay, which was also known as Pineapple Quay after an inn which once flourished close by, was the busiest. Recently restored, this small grassy quay stands on a still bend of the creek surrounded by low slopes of fields and trees, where the mutter of a tractor mingles with the calls of wading birds.

The marsh to the south of the quay was once a small creek flowing up towards the wonderfully named village of Botus Fleming. John Batt of Moditonham began damming the creek in the 1760s and created a fertile meadow below his house; a move which Gilbert, writing in 1817, con-sidered wise because of 'the nauseous smell which arose from the mud at the going out of the tide'.

Botus Fleming should not be missed: a quiet and scattered village in the depths of old fruit-growing country, where the gravestones in the churchyard bear names like Summerfield, Orchard and Garland. The village pub is legendary. Long famed for its dignified skill in fending off the 20th century, the Rising Sun is still successfully holding out in splendid, fusty isolation.

## Landulph

At the entrance to Kingsmill Lake on its northern shore, and almost hidden behind a broad and silent expanse of marshland, you will find the churchtown of Landulph, an ancient holy place and a long-forgotten port. Landulph is close to perfection; nothing jars the eye or ear. It has an extraordinary stillness, and the wildness of the marsh seems to swallow sound and exude an air of mystery.

Until about 150 years ago this marsh, a paradise for birds, was a tidal inlet called the Goodlake; then Rector Arundell of Landulph built the high embankment across the mouth in order to convert it to rich pasture-land (perhaps inspired by the success of John Batt) as part of his great plan to develop Landulph as a fashionable spa. Arundell's scheme broke him, however, before it reached fruition, and although parishioners today can remember walking on firm pastureland and crossing the drainage channels on little wooden bridges, it was not very long before the land began to revert to river, and slipped gently into willow carr and marshland.

In the days when the Goodlake used to flow up to the churchyard walls, and the rector had often to be ferried by boat from rectory to church, Landulph was a port in its own right with its own fleet of sea-going vessels. Even more surprisingly, in the 15th century, this became one of the Southwest's main embarkation points on the pilgrim route to Spain. Santiago de Compostella was the destination; the tomb of St James, about which the town had grown, became in the Middle Ages the third most important Christian place of pilgrimage after Jerusalem and Rome. The devout and the penitent flocked there from Britain, despite the gruelling and hazardous journey, and in 1434 at least 160 of the 2,460 pilgrims issued with licences sailed from the little port of Landulph.

The other surprising thing about Landulph is that the church contains the tomb of Theodore Paleologus, a descendant of the Christian Emperors of Constantinople, who died at Clifton in this parish in 1636. Two centuries later, Penaluna wrote, with a rather grisly detachment: 'The vault having been opened about 50 years since, the body of Paleologus was found in an oak coffin, in so perfect a state, that the features could be distinguished. He appeared to be above the common height, with an oval countenance, aquiline nose, and a white beard of considerable length.' The family tie between Paleologus and the Duke of Edinburgh helped to bring about the Royal visit to Landulph Church and parish on July 25, 1962.

## Cargreen

Just upstream from the mouth of the Tavy, with its railway bridge like a defensive chain slung across from bank to bank, and its magnificent backdrop of distant Dartmoor, the village of Cargreen clusters tightly around its little rocky point on the Cornish bank of the Tamar. There has been an inevitable spread back and outwards, but nothing can detract from the charm of old Cargreen, dominated by the splendid 1830s steam-driven bone crushing mill which is now an industrious boatyard.

Like Landulph, Cargreen was once the home port for sea-going ships, and even after its glory days were over it remained one of the most important quays on this great tidal thoroughfare. One of the Tamar's ancient ferry crossings used to run between Cargreen Quay and a causeway off Thorn Point on the Devon bank. The causeway was built out through the mud, and a flagpole erected on which intending passengers could hoist a red flag to summon the ferryboat.

## UP TO PENTILLIE

Just upriver from Thorn Point there is a secret inlet protected by a labyrinth of saltings known as Egypt Bay. Liphill Quay lies hidden deep within this at the northern end of the saltings, yet it used to be regularly visited by small barges which could thread their way through the maze of little creeks.

From here onwards there is a string of old quays on the Devon bank, of which only Weir Quay is still used. Little remains to be seen of Clamoak Quay; but 300 yards upriver you can still make out the wharf, now grown with furze and reeds, which served the once-prosperous South Tamar silver–lead mine. The mine was abandoned after the 1856 disaster when the river broke into the underwater galleries (no one was killed, it being a Sunday evening). All that remains is a pale scar in the green hillside and a chimney peeping out of the trees; overhead the pylons stride unnoticing.

At Cleave, ruined limekilns and pretty houses stand by the old hard; and then a mass of masts heralds the surprisingly unspoilt Weir Quay. This deep-water berth was associated from earliest times with the ancient silver–lead mines of the Bere Alston peninsula (which have been worked on and off since about 1290), and in the last century it became one of the leading centres for smelting the ores. Eighteen furnaces were worked by 80 or 90 men, and the quay was improved to take vessels of up to 400 tons. Hole's Hole, just a little upriver, with its fine old limekilns and sturdy quay, is also an ancient river port, associated with the fruit and flower trade as well as with the mines. Beneath the tree-grown cliffs here, and elsewhere on the river, you might see salmon fishermen at work in their long, low, brightly coloured rowing-boats, netting with the techniques and skills of their ancestors.

Beyond South Hooe, site of one of the two richest mines of the Bere Peninsula (the other being the South Tamar) and also the site of another ancient ferry crossing which ran to the quay at Clifton on the Cornish bank (the skeleton of which can still be discerned), the Tamar begins one of its characteristically exaggerated loops. 'The surging snake/Has not more folds than Tamar', wrote Carrington in the 1830s, and this particular fold is so deep that the farms of North and South Hooe, separated by a mere 400 yards on land, are nearly 2½ miles apart by river.

## Pentillie

Beyond Clifton the high, mysterious woods of Pentillie rise ahead, and here again is that charm of contrasting banks, for the Devon shore is a low expanse of marsh and reeds on the inside of the bend. Perched on a promontory high above its quay, swaddled in Carrington's 'noble massiness of leafage' is the splendid Gothic castle of Pentillie, built for an 18th century adventurer named James Tillie by W. Wilkins (who also built Tregothnan on the Truro River).

Behind the castle and high up on Mount Ararat with its scalp of trees is a mausoleum wherein, as an old story goes, a previous Tillie who was a fanatical atheist directed his executors to place his body, fully dressed and sitting on a chair with 'tobacco, pipes and liquor' on the table before him in readiness for his imminent return to life.

## PENTILLIE QUAY

The quay today exudes the same forbidding air of privacy as the whole estate, but in the last century refreshments were offered to passing voyagers, and it was also one of the regular stops on the market run.

The market boat made the trip on Tuesdays, Thursdays and Saturdays, leaving Calstock at six in the morning and calling at Cotehele Quay, Halton Quay, Pentillie, Hole's Hole or Weir Quay, Cargreen and Saltash, and arriving at Northcorner Pontoon, for Devonport market, at nine. The run was taken over by paddle steamers in the mid-19th century, at a time when the river was at its most crowded with schooners, sailing barges and steamers. An intense rivalry developed between the different steamship companies trying to run the fastest trips and attract the most custom, and it sometimes led to violent encounters. In March 1866, for instance, the captain of the 70 foot *Wellington* was indicted for having 'wilfully and maliciously run into the steamer *Ariel*'.

## Halton Quay

Pentillie Quay never served much more than the farms on the estate, but Halton Quay, just upriver, was among the busiest on the Tamar. Now it is one of the most silent, most peaceful places imaginable; just a tiny row of cottages, huge overgrown limekilns, and a simple chapel in the old coal store and clerk of works' office—a plain white building like a child's drawing. The only sounds are of reeds rustling in their beds all around the old quay, the occasional splosh of a salmon jumping, and the constant sipping of water on the shore. There is an unusual amount of sky here; it is a place with low horizons and room to breathe, so different from the close seclusion of most river valleys.

A little way beyond the chapel and cottages a long low house stands at right angles to the lane, surrounded by flowers. This used to be the Malsters Arms until it closed in 1890, some time before the quay lost its custom. In its heyday Halton Quay supported a timber business and store, making punnets and boxes for the local fruit and flower trade, a coal depot, a granary, a malt-house and kiln, an ore yard, and a corn mill as well as the inn, and the limekilns (considered today the most impressive on the river) which burned lime until 1916. The corn mill worked fitfully in the 1930s but was demolished soon afterwards. By the beginning of the last war, coal deliveries to the quay had come to an end and the barges and steamers no longer called.

The ferry which used to run to North Hooe, snug under the hill, an ancient passage leading into the heart of the old mining district, is also just another memory. Hearder who wrote his enchanting *Guide to the Tamar* after voyaging upriver in a rowing boat in 1841, came upon it '. . . the boat . . . passed us as we glided up the stream, it contained a solitary passenger, who was sitting with his legs extended in a horizontal position across the seats, the bottom of the boat containing a black-looking pool of stagnant water; the rower was a thick-set country lad, who seemed as much at ease in this queer amalgamation of decayed wood and rusty nails as though he had been enjoying a comfortable lounge on a pillow of down; the boat had been considered a good one ever since his father could recollect and it would ill become him to find fault with such a trustworthy and long-tried servant'.

Between Halton Quay and Cotehele Quay, the Devon bank is steeper and wilder, dotted with farm hards and patches of woodland and the odd mine stack, while, opposite, Cornwall's garden parish of St Dominick drops to the Tamar in striped hillsides and broad sweeps of reed beds. Many of the parish's fields are still, like these, a softly coloured mosaic of flowers and vegetables, but most of the once-famous orchards have disappeared and the old skills been lost or replaced.

## Cotehele Quay

Cotehele Quay, still 'environed by limekilns' as it was in Hearder's day, presents perhaps the loveliest collection of buildings on the river in a remote and sylvan setting. The name Cotehele means 'the wood on the estuary', and the woods here are particularly thick and fine, stretching along the Tamar and up the Morden valley for nearly a mile. The quay, the woods, a corn mill in the Morden valley, and the village of Bohetherick to the south all belong to the National Trust as part of the 1289 acre Cotehele estate.

Cotehele Quay has been thoughtfully preserved, and, moored alongside the old lime quay, there is the *Shamrock*, a beautifully restored Tamar sailing barge whose story is told in the granary museum.

In the mid-19th century there were seven working limekilns here, along with the granary, manure stores, several ore yards, coal stores, a timber yard, the inn, a brewery and malt-house, a salt store, stables, labourers' cottages and 'an excellent Dwelling-House and Garden'. Apart from the usual river cargoes landed and loaded at most of the Tamar quays— limestone, seasand and 'dock dung' (sweepings from Plymouth streets), coal, timber, grain, copper ore, arsenic, soft fruit and vegetables—this also served as a general port for a wide area, and most of the supplies for the booming mining town of Callington, five miles inland, were drawn from here. Inevitably, there was also a ferry crossing from here to the Devon bank: those Tamar quays which pre-date the Industrial Revolution usually began life as old river crossing points.

137

*'. . . perhaps the loveliest collection of buildings on the river . . .'*

## COTEHELE HOUSE

The house itself, of which Carew wrote that 'the buildings are ancient, large, strong and fair', can be reached by a delightful walk upriver through the woods, or directly up the driveway from the quay, or by heading up the Morden valley towards the mill and climbing the wooded valley side. The first route leads you past the perfect little 15th century chapel, perched on a rock above the river, inside which a plaque tells the story of Sir Richard Edgcumbe's dramatic escape into the Tamar here, which led to the building of the chapel. The path then turns up through the luxuriant valley garden (a riot of streams and flowers and shrubs tumbling towards the Tamar) and past the medieval dovecote, cool and dark inside and filled with the rumbling of doves.

Cotehele is the ancestral home of the Edgcumbe family and one of the least altered medieval houses in the country; it is a gloriously snug jumble of cobbled courtyards, mullioned windows and wonderful great chimneys. Despite the fact that this is such a popular place to visit, it has the peace found only in very old houses; visitors walk slowly, talk softly, and are visibly disconcerted when a jet tearing overhead bursts rudely into the 16th century.

### Calstock

When approached by water, Calstock seems surprisingly large after the remote unpeopled miles of Tamar. The elegant viaduct lends a splendour to the scene of unusually tall, white, rough-walled houses climbing the steep hillside for all as though this were any Cornish fishing harbour; it is easy to forget that Calstock is about fourteen miles inland, by water.

In Saxon times Calstock was an important river quay and it has ruled the Tamar, along with Morwellham and Saltash, ever since. For many centuries this parish and thus the river port have been associated with tin mining.

It was copper, discovered in the area in the 1770s, which brought Calstock its most prosperous years until it failed in the late 19th century. Quays used to start right down at the Ashburton Hotel (built in 1859 to cater for the increased river traffic), now the Danescombe Valley Hotel with white lattice balcony and splashes of geraniums and sweet peas, and protected by the National Trust. The quays stretched upriver for nearly a mile to the copper ore yard; most of this old yard is now a recreation ground and you can still see some granite kerbing marking the horse-drawn tramway which served the quays.

After 1872 the quays were connected to the East Cornwall Mineral Railway which ran from Calstock inland to Kelly Bray through the heart of rich mining and quarrying land. For its first half mile or so the railway was worked as an incline using the counterbalance principle, with the help of a stationary engine at the top of the hill. The bridge where the incline crossed the road near its beginning is still standing, a little way upriver from the Danescombe Valley Hotel and alongside one of Calstock's many sets of limekilns. There are some more kilns just back towards Calstock from here; surrounded by a garden, they have vines growing up their walls and runner beans on their roof. The track of the incline on the river side of the bridge has been obscured by a new house, but you can see it on the other side of the road through the trees, labouring up the steep valley side. Some remains of the old incline station at the top of the hill, including the water tower and wagon repair shed, can still be seen to the south of the Calstock–Danescombe road. Copper ore, arsenic, bricks and granite formed the bulk of the river-bound traffic on the railway. At the foot of the incline a horse collected the wagons and drew them to the various quayside berths: the copper, for instance, went all the way along to the ore yard while the granite was mostly shipped from the Danescombe end. The horse would return to the foot of the incline with burnt lime and imported loads of coal, grain, manure and timber for distribution inland.

With the completion of the viaduct in 1908, which connected the Kelly Bray line with Bere Ferrers and the line to Plymouth (bypassing Calstock and the incline), the fate of Calstock as a port and the Tamar as a working river was sealed, although death came slowly. However, Calstock would have suffered much earlier when the copper mines failed, as did Morwellham, had it not had so many other resources to fall back upon. Within the parish there were papermills, brick and tile works, many granite quarries, a tannery, a brewery and foundry, and Calstock-made rope was famous for miles around. The traditional fruit cultivation of the Tamar Valley prospered too, even in as industrial a parish as Calstock, and was greatly encouraged by the new railway connections.

Between 1880 and the First World War it was shipbuilding which kept Calstock busy and famous, thanks in particular to the yard of the Goss Brothers. It was little more than a mud bank on the Devon side of the river (the old tin-roofed shack just upriver from the viaduct is all that remains today), and yet it turned out many fine boats and ships, including the 150 ton *Garlandstone*, the last ketch to be launched on the Tamar. The Goss family also used to run the Calstock ferry during their time at the yard. This crossing was one of the oldest on the river but it no longer operates. Ferry Farm on the Devon bank, just upriver from the Goss's old shed, used to be the Passage Inn, then the green hillside behind it was thick with cherry orchards, and the cattle-grazed meadows and reed beds in front of the inn were pleasure grounds where strawberry and cream teas and children's swings in a rose garden attracted tourist parties off the steamers.

Hearder's 'hill of toilsome ascent' leads up to Calstock's parish church of St Andrew. Even if you do not care for the clinically neat churchyard, with its anonymous green mounds, it is still worth reading some of the carved slate headstones stacked around the churchyard wall, which chronicle the many mining tragedies of the last century.

## Upriver from Calstock

Beyond Calstock the Tamar performs another of its great loops, travelling 3½ miles before returning to a point just 300 yards from Calstock Church; the river ceases to be navigable 1¼ miles beyond this, at Weir Head.

This last stretch of waterway winds through the great mining and industrial heartland of the last century, one of the most fascinating of Cornwall's many old industrial areas, which is now a silent, remote country of old chimneys and thick undergrowth with the Tamar almost lost in the wilderness. John Lloyd Warden Page wrote tetchily in 1893 that 'Hardly do we leave Calstock Quay when those abominations, the mines, begin to disfigure the riverside'.

### THE DEVON QUAYS

If the Devon bank of the river captures the prize for scenic beauty from now on, it also has most of the quays and industrial remains. Cornwall can offer Okeltor Quay, built to serve Okel Tor Mine—a lead, copper and arsenic mine opened in 1848 and clearly identified today by its chimney stacks, ruined buildings, and waste dumps scattered on the hillside among thick gorse, heather and birch trees. The old path between mine and quay still has a public right of way and makes a fascinating walk.

Devon, however, has a whole string of old quays: Butspill and Tuckermarsh, both with their white houses and probably medieval but transformed by the brief prosperity of mines; Rumleigh farm quay; the Rumleigh brickworks quay (their prominent stack, opposite Okel Tor, looks a little ropey these days); and the substantial quays at Gawton where

*Morwellham Quay—'. . . no better evocation of life in a 19th century river port . . .'*

nearly 350 people used to live and work. This, little more than a farm quay in the 18th century, was enlarged to take surplus ore from Devon Great Consols and to serve the newly reopened Gawton Mine which went on to become the leading arsenic producer in the district. Gawton's mine dumps are still conspicuous on the Devon bank above Rumleigh brickworks: ochrous mounds, ominously bald among the riot of bushes and underwood. You can also still make out the remains of the arsenic flue (built in the 1890s, over 6 feet high in places and said to be the longest of its kind in the country) winding up the hillside to the gently leaning chimney stack, high up in the woods above. Men working in Gawton's King's Shaft, under the river, could hear the thump-thump of paddle wheels above their heads as steamers passed up to Weir Head and back.

New Quay, further on, was also developed from a humble farm quay because of the enormous output of Devon Great Consols, a mine which was not discovered until 1845, which transformed the Tamar Valley, and which was for nearly twenty years the richest copper mine in Europe.

There is no better evocation of life in a 19th century river port than at Morwellham Quay, just around the corner from New Quay. This ancient trading place was serving as Tavistock's port in 1105, and continued to increase in importance until, by the last century, it had become the busiest inland port in Devon and Cornwall. Monopolized by Devon Great Consols from the 1840s onwards, its fortunes soared with the mine's, and then plummeted irreversibly when the mine closed at the turn of the century, although it was still used for a while by local barge traffic. Today it is one of the most successful of all the Southwest's tourist attractions.

Beyond Morwellham the Tamar sidles under the towering Morwell Rocks, the destination for many a Victorian excursion because of the view from the top.

By the notoriously sharp Impham Turn there used to be a quay on the Devon bank; and Netstakes Quay, once a successful shipyard, was on the Cornish side just by the last turn before Weir Head.

Weir Head marks the end of navigation on the Tamar today, but for over a century up to the 1930s the weir could be bypassed via a canal, known as the Tamar Manure Navigation because small barges carrying manure, sand, limestone or coal were its main traffic. The grand, decaying lockgates are still there, as is the lock-keeper's cottage, but the canal company went into liquidation soon after the last war after decades of gradual dilapidation. The old towpath makes a glorious walk up to the massive limekilns which mark the highest point reached by the barges, and beyond to the fine 16th century New Bridge which for 430 years or so was the lowest road-bridge on the Tamar, carrying one of the three main old routes into Cornwall. On the way you will pass the sites of many industries: the Bealswood Brickworks, all gone now, occupied a vast area of land behind the row of cottages on the canal bank; the sites of a large gasworks and two quarries are further on; and above, sprawling on the hillside, is Gunnislake, a town which was founded and prospered on the fortunes of one venture, the Gunnislake Old Mine.

# Index

## South Coast Harbours

A useful guide to further reading on the areas covered by this book is available from the publisher. Please include return postage.